PN
1992.8   MacDonald, J. Fred
.W4
M33   Who shot the
1987   Sheriff?

DATE DUE

SIDNEY B. COULTER LIBRARY
Onondaga Community College
Syracuse, New York 13215

WHO SHOT THE SHERIFF?

Media and Society Series
J. Fred MacDonald, *General Editor*

WHO SHOT THE SHERIFF?
The Rise and Fall
of the Television Western

J. Fred MacDonald

PRAEGER

New York
Westport, Connecticut
London

Library of Congress Cataloging-in-Publication Data

MacDonald, J. Fred.
  Who shot the Sheriff?

  (Media and society)
  Bibliography: p.
  Includes index.
  1. Westerns (Television programs) – United States.
I. Title. II. Series.
PN1992.8.W4M33 1987   791.45′09′093278   86-18230
ISBN 0-275-92326-6 (alk. paper)
ISSN 0890-7161

Copyright © 1987 by Praeger Publishers

Library of Congress Catalog Card Number: 86-18230
ISBN: 0-275-92326-6
ISSN 0890-7161

First published in 1987

Praeger Publishers, 521 Fifth Avenue, New York, NY 10175
A division of Greenwood Press, Inc.

Printed in the United States of America

The paper used in this book complies with the Permanent
Paper Standard issued by the National Information Standards
Organization (Z39.48-1984).

10 9 8 7 6 5 4 3 2 1

For my aunt and uncle—Marion C. and William J. MacDonald—settlers in the post-World War II "Wild West" who eventually returned East . . . but who still love the Western.

Contents

List of Tables

Preface

The history of the Western on television is without precedent. No form of mass entertainment has been so dominant and then so insignificant as the Western. Where once hoofbeats and six-guns were a familiar part of prime-time diversion, they and the other accouterments of the genre are found now only in syndicated reruns, rare feature films, and occasional made-for-TV movies. Where in the 1960s media sociologist Marshall McLuhan could contend that spiritually Americans then were living in *Bonanza*-land, contemporary society evidences no fascination with the symbolism and mystique of the video Old West.

That the TV Western is dead is obvious. It is statistically verifiable that when Westerns are televised not enough viewers are interested. It is also plain that by the late 1980s the three major networks avoid them because viewer disinterest has been evident for almost two decades. What is not clear, however, is why Americans have rejected the genre. What needs to be understood is how television viewers could have adored and then abandoned the Western so definitively. The book attempts to explain such a development.

U.S. network television is a business serving a mass audience via a mass medium. It is, however, a risky and competitive enterprise. By promising large numbers of viewers, networks attract as advertisers mass producers eager to sell to the mass market. Sponsors pay according to audience size. By delivering audiences larger than those of its competitors, a network is able to charge the highest advertising rates. For obvious reasons the networks are concerned with "selling" their programs to the public. Offerings that deliver a sufficient number of viewers are retained; those not attractive enough are terminated. In the case of the Western, however, it is not just a single program or a series that has failed—it is an entire genre and its failure has been chronic.

TV in the United States does not operate in a vacuum. It effects and is affected by the society it serves. Historically, successful programming is a matter of relevance that has been revealed in a mix of commercialism, social relevance, tastes that run in cycles, demographic influences, and sensitivities toward national political and cultural matters. If a program or genre is popular, its success is based on a relevant combination of these factors. Conversely, if a show or entertainment form is rejected by the mass audience, the cause of its demise can be found in these factors. When successful programming is on TV, Americans are on TV. Therefore, when treating the history of the video Western one is tracing not only the record of a genre, but the evolution of U.S. society during the past four decades.

The writing of popular cultural history is an elusive undertaking. Made for entertainment and profit, not scholarship, most of the products of popular culture are ephemeral, disposable, commercially unavailable, and otherwise not collected by university libraries or other research institutions. As a result, the study of television programming and its relationship to U.S. society is beset with technical problems. The researcher must use unconventional resources that are often difficult and expensive to obtain. Weekly TV logs, fan magazines, and trade newspapers become important tools. Scripts and tapes of soundtracks are helpful, but VTR recordings of vintage series—often televised at obscure hours on nonnetwork and cable stations—offer better insights into the past.

All of these sources have been used in this present study. Moreover, I have drawn heavily upon my sizable personal archive of filmed television programs. Where a source is verifiable in print, I have footnoted appropriately. Where resources are nonprint and privately held, I have cited in the text the dates of broadcast and other marks of identification.

This is the first offering in the new Media and Society series from Praeger Publishers. As such I hope this book suggests that modern scholarship may responsibly move away from a devotion to the publicly archived printed page and in the direction of nontraditional media that are often available only through untraditional research techniques. The history of the United States can no longer be gleaned only from print sources. As surely as the archeologist discovers the past through architectural remains, chards, oral tradition, and other nonprint artifacts, the student of American society must now embrace a variety of audio-visual materials in the search for understanding. Political, cultural, economic, social, and intellectual historians of the United States must make allowance in their methodologies and focuses for consideration of popular culture as a historical force.

There are several people I wish to thank for their assistance, both direct and indirect, in preparation of this book. Desta Elliott and John Dykla were important in helping me compose the manuscript. Their roles as midwife and "midhusband" to my birth as a word processor user were crucial. Thanks go also to the many film collectors across the nation whose love for TV film is preserving the history of the industry and American popular culture. Especially helpful were Larry Urbanski, Veto Stasiunaitis, Scott Zuniga, Andy Jaysnovitch, and Omer Whayne. Others who assisted by supplying tapes, related materials, and support include Les Waffen of the National Archives, Tom LaPorte, Michael Marsden, and Robert J. Thompson. Thanks also to my wife Leslie W. MacDonald who once again offered strategic advice and encouragement.

WHO SHOT THE SHERIFF?

1
Who Shot the Sheriff?

This is a history of cultural life and death on American television. As a consideration of the Western, it is a discussion of a socially relevant type of storytelling, a thriving cultural attraction whose symbols and rhetoric helped define American society for almost a century. As an investigation of the disappearance of that genre from network prime-time television, this is an inquiry into the flowering and withering of a mass diversion whose value-laden conventions were once a plentiful part of evening entertainment in the United States.

The Western arrived with the first TV sets in the late 1940s. From the outset it was well received; but for the Western to have been successful on television it had to have been culturally "acceptable" to the mass audience. As with other entertainment genres, the success of the video Western was based on a synchronization between qualities inherent within the genre and values relevant to American life at the time. In an era characterized by East-West confrontation and new national and international initiatives for the United States, the Western stories and symbols fit the temper of the time. Their political, military, social, economic, and spiritual implications were most appropriate. For a people seeking direction and justification, the Western offered purposeful explanations. Its overwhelming popularity was neither a fad nor a function of cyclical patterns of cultural taste. In an unprecedented manner the video Western captured the national imagination because many Americans understood themselves and their civilization in terms of the genre. Always a militaristic art form, the Western spoke especially well the language of Cold War America.

The failure of the genre on television in more recent years, therefore, raises serious questions. Has it temporarily passed out of favor, or has the TV Western permanently ceased to be relevant to Americans? If its video record for a long time has been dismal, who does it continue to appear, however limitedly, in formulaic novels, occasional feature films, and disastrously short-lived TV series? Was it undermined, as many are quick to conclude, by being overexposed on television, or was it destroyed by more profound shifts in the attitudes of its audience? If it is now dead as a popular art form, what does this imply for the moral and ideological messages traditionally communicated through the genre? Should the video Western now be considered an historic relic, or can it be revitalized and again contribute to the entertaining of mass America?

In treating such questions, this study becomes more than a nostalgic chronicle of a lost TV genre. Indeed, seeking to understand the demise of the television Western demands an analysis of the interrelationship between popular culture, television, and sociopolitical development in the United States during the past four decades.

THE SPIRIT OF THE WESTERN

The destruction of the Western as viable television fare was no inconsequential accomplishment. It was truly the all-American genre. No type of popular entertainment has been associated more completely with American civilization. Politically, spiritually, economically, and ethically the genre has communicated an understanding of the United States and its place in the world.

Historically, the Western has flourished in popular literature, film, radio, and especially television. The noted scholarly critic Leslie Fiedler traced its New World inspiration to Massachusetts as early as 1609.[1] For a nation seeking enduring social role models, the genre offered an array of frontier characters whose names and exploits remain legion. From embellished historical realities like Daniel Boone, Wyatt Earp, and Buffalo Bill to purely fictional types such as Natty Bumppo, Pecos Bill, and the Lone Ranger it has offered a pantheon of heroic activists as inspirational as they were entertaining.

The spirit of the Western has ingratiated itself into varied dimensions of American reality. It endures in the commercial names given to models of automobiles. High schools and universities adopt its terms to describe themselves. Professional sports franchises use its vocabulary to name their teams. Urban dwellers have been drawn to the leather boots and denim that are its clothing styles, and to country-western performers and songs that are its musical tastes.

Even recent national presidential administrations have found the mystique of the Western appropriate. John F. Kennedy christened his presidency "The New Frontier." Lyndon B. Johnson was more or less an authentic cowboy whose LBJ Ranch, situated on the banks of the Pedernales River in south-central Texas, became the alternate presidential residence throughout the mid-1960s.

Twice elected chief executive, Ronald Reagan formerly starred in cowboy movies such as *Santa Fe Trail* and *Cattle Queen of Montana*; and during the 1965-66 television season he hosted the Western series *Death Valley Days*. Even Dr. Henry A. Kissinger, the foreign relations advisor for Presidents Richard M. Nixon and Gerald R. Ford, understood himself as a frontiersman with portfolio. He characterized his diplomatic technique in terms of the heroic loner who rides to the rescue. "I've always acted alone," he told the Italian journalist Oriana Fallaci in 1972.

> Americans like that immensely. Americans like the cowboy who leads the wagon train by riding ahead alone on his horse, the cowboy who rides all alone into the town, the village, with his horse and nothing else. Maybe even without a pistol, since he doesn't shoot. He acts, that's all, by being in the right place at the right time. In short, a Western.[2]

The genre has exercised a significant influence on American society in the twentieth century. Despite the learned debunking of an intellect otherwise as perceptive as Henry Nash Smith, it has been considerably more than a vacuous form of amusement that has degenerated since its inception "to the near-juvenile level it was to occupy with virtually no change down to our own present day."[3] To the contrary, the Western has been hailed as an original art and cultural form sprung totally from U.S. civilization. Its mythic characters have been emulable types for generations. Its stories have offered timely justification for a society that at base remained a relatively pristine experiment in self-governance.

The Western possesses a classic formulation recognizable to all audiences. Here is the cowboy, frontiersman, or lawman operating on or near the furthest reaches of civilized life. Here is the cruel wilderness in which incipient American society struggles against adversity to survive and even flourish. The classic Western contains familiar ingredients: heroes and guns, horses, cattle, outlaws and Indians, and the like—usually situated in desert locales on the nineteenth-century U.S. frontier.

As with most entertainment classifications, however, there exist gray areas within the Western, places where the traditional formulation overlaps other genres. Here it meets and blends with such forms as situation comedy, adventure stories, and military dramas. In cases where the archetypes and themes of the Western dominate these relationships, the result is a modified, peripheral Western—but one that must be understood together with the classic relationship of the genre.

In television the hybrid Western constituted a small, but not insignificant, part of the totality. In *Hawkeye and the Last of the Mohicans*, for example, the West was located in upstate New York in the eighteenth century. In *Daniel Boone*, frontier heroics took place in the Kentucky backwoods at the time of the Revolutionary War. *Yancy Derringer* was set in New Orleans immediately following the Civil War. Alaska and the Canadian Yukon during the Gold Rush were locales for *Klondike, The Alaskans,* and *Sergeant Preston of the Yukon.*

Alias Smith and Jones added levity to the drama of the Old West, *The Rounders* offered humor in the new West, and *F Troop* and *Pistol 'n' Petticoats* burlesqued the genre. Series like *Stoney Burke, The Wide Country, Empire* and *The Yellow Rose* ranged into the contemporary West interpreting that area as a place where civilization now thrived, but where modern cowboys and ranchers faced challenges similar to those confronted by their pioneering ancestors.

For the most part this study focuses on those series with classic formats. Such programs constitute the vast majority of the Westerns shown on television. These were dramatic offerings inspired by fanciful notions of the historic West. Ironically, the West in actuality was little more than a geographic region explored, conquered, and assimilated in a short, distinct time. But for a nation built by self-motivated immigrants seeking personal betterment, the West, real or otherwise, always seemed to perpetuate the promise. Here was elbow room and a fresh start—a place to plant and to grow. For a nation fashioned by dreamers, the West was an antidote to crowded cities and failed careers, a refuge for the bold still seeking challenges, a spiritual and geographic last chance to make the dream come true.

This strategic relationship between the West and the American psyche was not a detection of modern academic analysis. Its earliest delineation was made in 1893 when Frederick Jackson Turner described the manner in which the frontier experience shaped the character of the United States and its citizenry. Among his contentions, Turner argued:

The result is that to the frontier the American intellect owes its striking characteristics. That coarseness and strength combined with acuteness and inquisitiveness; that practical, inventive turn of mind, quick to find expedients; that masterful grasp of material things, lacking in the artistic but powerful to effect great ends; that restless nervous energy; that dominant individualism, working for good and for evil, and withal that buoyance and exuberance which comes with freedom—these are the traits of the frontier, or traits called out elsewhere because of the existence of the frontier.[4]

In its own peculiar way, the West—through its chief vehicle of communication, the Western—has been the American affirmation of an ancient aspiration. Its tales envisioned the new Eden, the land of milk and honey lost by the Israelites, the idealized city limned from Plato to St. Augustine to Jefferson. With such an influential place in American civilization, indeed in world culture, its unimportance as a contemporary television format is all the more striking.

THE WESTERN AND AMERICAN CIVILIZATION

Hoping to understand better the civilization that produced and sustained the genre, scholars have analyzed the Western from many perspectives. It has been approached in terms of religion, militarism, sociology, anthropology, psychological symbolism, dialectical materialism, and assorted critical methodologies. In the richest dissection of its inner dimensions, literary critic John Cawelti has discerned a multiplicity of implications accounting for the popularity of the genre. He argues convincingly in *The Six-Gun Mystique* that the Western possesses social, political, psychological, artistic, sociological, anthropological, and other qualities that make it misleading to focus too narrowly when seeking its meaning. Certainly, Cawelti was on target when he contended that

the Western's capacity to accommodate many different kinds of meaning—the archetypal pattern of heroic myth, the need for social ritual and for the disguised expression of latent motives and tensions—as well as its ability to respond to changing cultural themes and concerns—have made the formula successful as popular art and entertainment over many generations.[5]

Cawelti's eclectic approach, however, fails to answer the fundamental questions posited by this study. If the genre is so vital to American culture, so adaptable to changing times, and so chronically popular, why is it no longer accepted by the mass audience as a video entertainment form? It lives in the lusty writings of Louis L'Amour. It survives, albeit sparingly, in the modern films of actors such as Clint Eastwood, Gene Hackman, and Charles Bronson. The Western motif may appear occasionally in TV commercials, exploited to sell hamburgers, candy, and the like. Moreover, it still captures the imagination of cultural scholars. On television, however, the most popular medium, the weekly entertainment forum for hundreds of millions of viewers, the genre is moribund. If it is dead on TV, is it not dead as an idiom of social importance?

In seeking to understand why the Western perished on American television, the most profitable line of inquiry is that which appreciates the sociopolitical implications of the genre. Here, analysts have rightfully suggested that since the stories and iconography of the Western deal perforce with an historic reality, their connotations possess a significance that is both topical and enduring. Attesting to the relevant emphases within the genre, Philip French in his study of Western feature films actually discerned four types of Westerns. These were the "Kennedy Western," the "Johnson Western," the "Buckley Western," and the "Goldwater Western." As French explained it in the 1960s, these typologies had critical differences that more or less matched the policies and social philosophies of new-liberal John F. Kennedy, old-liberal Lyndon B. Johnson, new-conservative William F. Buckley, and old-conservative Barry Goldwater.[6]

With more precision and depth John H. Lenihan traced the Western film as it adapted to shifting historical forces in the decades after World War II. In explaining the ways in which the genre incorporated themes of the Cold War, the struggle for racial equality, and the alienated condition of modern mankind trapped in urban and technological anonymity, he argued in *Showdown* for the vitality and basic adaptability of the Western. "There is no demonstrable reason why the Western should be less appropriate for today's audiences than it was for those of yesterday," Lenihan maintained in 1980. He concluded, romantically as well as optimistically, that the genre's "proved capacity for redefining America's mythic heritage in contemporary terms would suggest, even during the current period of its quiescence, that the Western is an unlikely candidate for cultural oblivion."[7]

The critique of the Western offered by Jenni Calder was a vigorous defense of the genre as an historically American phenomenon with implications for the world. In *There Must Be a Lone Ranger*, this

British scholar in 1975 focused principally on Western movies and concluded that the genre was indestructible—at least hopefully so. "It is likely that the Western myth will survive, and will survive on many different levels," she asserted.

> It enriches a brief past for the benefit of a barren present. It feeds contemporary culture, and has done so for many years, with a vision of independence which America and the world find both comforting and exciting. It can suggest anarchy, rebellion, as well as the most offensive acts of nationalism. It can emphasize the uniqueness of a nation and the inviolability of the individual. It can provide simultaneously an escape and a challenge. All this is arguably dangerous mental pablum for a nation that is inactive on its own ground and overactive on the territory of others, but with so much to offer the Western myth is, hopefully, invulnerable.[8]

Anticipating structuralist thought on the matter, John W. Evans argued perceptively in an essay in 1962 that the Western, especially as evidenced by its proliferation on television, represented a psychosocial answer to the oppressive qualities of modern society, a society marked by the decline of close relationships, the deterioration of accepted norms, and the gradual shrinking of the individual's sphere of choice. The basic appeal of the genre, Evans contended, "lies in the fact that it is an invitation to escape to—or better, participate in —a world in which psychological gratifications are an almost perfect antidote to the alienated conditions of life in modern industrial society."[9] Still, however, Evans saw the Western as socially robust, a salubrious mechanism with an apparently bright future.

More than a decade later, from his perspective as a structuralist historian cognizant of the complex linkages between American civilization and its cultural products, Will Wright reached provocative conclusions. He suggested that the Western had come to reflect and support fundamental alterations in postindustrial capitalist society. In *Six Guns and Society*, he argued that the emergence of the modern technological state—with its emphases on specialization, social control, and power as wielded by elitists who placed group loyalty above obedience to law or altruistic social pursuit—had effectively destroyed the archetypal Western.

The story of the individualist-hero using physical strength and moral courage to rescue innocents from malefactors, in Wright's view, had given way to the corporate champion—the professional hero who operated as an autonomous actor while finding purpose and satisfaction as part of an elite power group—who worked for money and acted out the bogus individualism of the technocratic society where systems of mass production and mass consumption must suppress individuality in favor of the mass market.

Despite an apparent distaste for the new form, Wright remained optimistic about the viability of the genre. In his view, if modern humanity found power and meaning in belonging to or envying influential elites, the acceptable Western need only reflect the values of this structural realignment. For him the new Western only had to highlight the professional hero whose prowess "depends more on technical strength and less on strength of character"; who "does much less standing up for ideas or principles and much more proving of his technical skills as a fighter"; and who "by joining the group and accepting the values of technical proficiency . . . shows himself to be superior to the petty, dull, weak people in ordinary society."[10]

Despite the appreciative and optimistic themes found in most scholarship on the Western, there have been voices offering contrary interpretations. As early as 1967 Larry McMurtry, a novelist whose works include *The Last Picture Show* and *Horseman, Pass By*, the book upon which the feature film *Hud* was based, suggested that the Western was headed for oblivion. Drawing upon the literary theories of critics such as Robert Warshow and Northrop Frye, he wrote of the genre: "The appeal cannot last forever . . . since the West definitely has been won, the cowboy must someday fade." McMurtry suggested that the Western would fall victim to certain cultural and social transformation already under way. "It is clear that the figure of the westerner is being replaced by more modern figures, principally that of the secret agent," he argued. To McMurtry, demographic shifts from rural to urban foreshadowed the demise of the Western. "An urban age demands an urban figure," he maintained, and "the secret agent, like the westerner a sort of insider-outsider, is an updated type of gunfighter. The secret agent has appropriated the style of the gunfighter and has added urbanity and cosmopolitanism."[11]

Writing almost two decades later, two foreign critics proclaimed the death of the filmic Western. After tracing the history of the filmic genre in *The Life and Times of the Western Movie*, the British writer Joe Hyams concluded that the end of the Western was proven in the fact that neither the popularity of Ronald Reagan, a politically conservative president, nor the urban cowboy craze of the early 1980s did anything to reinvigorate the Western film. "To the strains of country-and-western music," he contended, "the heads of studios—

studios owned by conglomerates interested only in finding 'this year's Star Wars'—casually agreed that the westerns were dead. No one seemed to believe in the West anymore."[1][2]

In *Le western*, published in 1982, the French film scholar Christian Viviani asserted that "the genre such as it is, is dead." For him, the demise was evolutionary, the end result of diversification in thematic content, of aging Western stars who were never replaced, and of changes in the studio system in the years after World War II. As Viviani understood these developments, the death of the Western was more a matter of artistic and business forces than sociopolitical developments.

> The Western is dead as a genre. The structure of the genre was tied to a production arrangement now obsolete. The era of five or six Westerns per month has ended. Certainly every now and then a filmmaker returns to the original sources and recaptures, as if by enchantment, the right balance . . . but the genre nowadays is finished.[13]

Those arguments declaring the Western dead have done little more than open the discussion. McMurtry was correct to link support for the genre with demographic and cultural developments, yet he needed to tie the Western to other aspects of American life, most notably changes in political, moral, military, religious, and psychological attitudes during the past several decades. Hyams failed to offer a thorough argument explaining why the Western died, and why neither the urban cowboy craze nor the nostalgic political conservatism of the Reagan presidency were unable to reinvigorate the genre. Likewise, Viviani's perspective as a student of the art of cinema offered no satisfying reasons for the demise of the Western. In mourning the passing of the genre as a function of industry decline instead of audience taste, Viviani focused on effect rather than cause.

Few analysts of the Western have given the genre sufficient attention as a powerful communicator of political values, and, as such, as a baromoter of American popular thinking. Yet, in its archetypes, symbols, story lines, and historical interpretation, the genre of a century has presented a ritualized reaffirmation of American prerogatives. In foreign nations the Western may be appreciated as a compelling adventure or probing human drama, but in the United States it has always had a political undertone offering a philosophy of right and wrong with personal, national, and international implications.

It was no coincidence that during the first Reagan administration the Congress of the United States ordered a medal struck honoring

John Wayne—the first medal minted to commemorate a movie actor —for his filmic embodiment of the American character. In his movies, and especially in his Westerns, John Wayne by that time represented a stereotyped view of the American as strong, assertive, and resourceful; dedicated to the concept of individualism and its economic corollary, the free enterprise system; and nationalistic, even jingoistic, in his support for the United States. In sum, his movie image epitomized conservative American political thinking by the early 1980s.

Importantly, too, none of these interpreters of the genre have focused with analytical depth on the Western as it appeared on television. Yet, for decades TV offered countless thousands of Westerns with their relentless mix of adventure and political values. Their enticing message was communicated most effectively, entering the privacy of living rooms, bedrooms, dens, and other areas where families and individuals relaxed in the informality of their homes. A Gallup poll in January 1963 revealed that two-thirds of the nation watched Westerns on TV. Ironically, the same survey indicated that more than half the population of the United States had not gone to a movie during the entire preceding year.[14]

For its part, the public was a willing customer for television. By 1960 there were video receivers in 89.4 percent of the households in the United States. More than electric toasters, washing machines, automobiles, or vacuum cleaners, people owned TV sets. Demand remained strong, too, as manufacturers between 1959 and 1961 produced 6 million units annually. Americans devoured the medium. In 1961 the average household each day watched TV for 5 hours and 22 minutes. That year at any minute between 7 A.M. and 1 A.M. almost 14 million homes—representing 29.6 percent of all receivers in the nation—had a television set turned on. In the evening hours, between 6 P.M. and 1 A.M., that figure was even higher. At that time receivers were operating in more than 21 million homes, accounting for 44.9 percent of all sets in the nation.[15]

If they owned and operated video receivers, Americans also trusted what they saw. Surveys in the 1950s and 1960s demonstrated a burgeoning belief in what was televised. In 1959 respondents to a Roper poll rated TV stations far ahead of local government in terms of the quality of the job being done. When asked in the same poll which communications medium they would most want to save, respondents placed television first at 42 percent, far ahead of newspapers, radio, and magazines. By November 1963, TV surpassed newspapers as the most believable source of information—36 percent for TV compared to 24 percent for newspapers. Six years later the margin was even wider, 44 percent calling TV the "most reliable" news medium while only 21 percent named newspapers.[16]

As well as a trusted informant, television quickly became the principal medium of entertainment in the United States. For example, the effect of video upon Western commercial movies—whether first-rate features, B films, multi-chaptered serials, or two-reel shorts—was devastating. Of the 3,372 commercial Westerns made in the period 1930-77, more than 64 percent of the total appeared in the first two decades—more than 82 percent in the years before the emergence of adult-oriented TV Westerns in 1955. As statistics in Table 1 suggest, with the coming of television, the Western feature film practically ceased to exist.

It is a major oversight for analysts of American culture or politics to disregard the historical importance of television, and specifically the rise and fall of the video Western. Television is more influential and more indicative of popular thought than feature film, yet TV studies are scarce—and even frowned upon by some—while the consideration of motion pictures has become an accepted aspect of modern scholarly inquiry. Twenty years ago, however, Richard E. Peck in a pioneering essay suggested that the key to understanding the times rested now in the analysis of television programming. His observation remains valid.

> A work of art becomes in the hands of an historian, an artifact, a primary document which he uses to define the culture that produced it. Developments in literature, in the plastic arts, even in handicrafts, somehow help the archaeologist or historian to understand the minds and opinions of

TABLE 1   Western Commercial Films, 1930-77

Period	Total	% of Total
1930-41	1345	39.8
1942-45	412	12.2
1946-49	423	12.8
1950-55	592	17.5
1956-59	244	7.2
1960-69	203	6.0
1970-77	153	4.5

Source: Les Adams and Buck Rainey, *Shoot-em-ups. The Complete Reference Guide to Westerns of the Sound Era* (New Rochelle, NY: Arlington House, 1978).

the people whose concerns foster them. If such an approach is valid, and I think it is, consider then the delights awaiting some future historian who turns his attention to tapes of films of today's television fare. For television—not the plastic arts, not literature, not theater, not cinema—is the characteristic art form of the 1960s.[17]

Throughout most scholarship on the Western there has been an appreciative and optimistic theme. Even when intimating that such optimism rested more on wishful thinking than substance, most critics have been fans and most have predicted a limitless future for the genre. Yet, if the performance of the Western on television is the standard by which to assess the popularity and the future of the genre, the conclusions of these scholars need scrutiny.

On TV the Western had an unusual career. For the first quarter-century of the medium, it was an essential, often dominant, force in network programming. In its earliest manifestations the cowboy drama was primarily a juvenile phenomenon, carrying into network video a stunted understanding of the genre that was manifested also on network radio.

Ironically, when NBC, ABC, and CBS in the mid-1950s finally did commit themselves to Westerns intended for adult audiences—a move made in feature films almost two decades earlier—the Western attained unprecedented popularity and shaped TV programming for years.

Finally, in the wake of its overwhelming acceptance, the Western entered a period of retreat and popular rejection. By the 1970s the genre ceased to relate to TV audiences. By the 1980s it was dead. However, this was a period not without significant attempts to resuscitate the genre.

By considering the TV Western in its several historic phases, one can obtain a clearer picture of its importance to television, society, history, and culture. Moreover, such inquiry facilitates an understanding of the relationship between mass entertainment and political and social development in the United States.

NOTES

1. Leslie A. Fiedler, *The Return of the Vanishing American* (New York: Stein and Day, 1968), pp. 50-51.

2. Oriana Fallaci, *Interview with History* (Boston: Houghton Mifflin, 1976), p. 41.

3. Henry Nash Smith, *Virgin Land: The American West as Symbol and Myth* (Cambridge, Mass.: Harvard University Press, 1950), pp. 134-35.

4. Frederick Jackson Turner, *The Frontier in American History* (New York: Henry Holt, 1947), p. 37.

5. John G. Cawelti, *The Six-Gun Mystique*, 2nd ed. (Bowling Green, Ohio: Popular Press, 1984), p. 113.

6. Philip French, *Westerns: Aspects of a Movie Genre* (New York: Viking Press, 1973), pp. 28-40.

7. John H. Lenihan, *Showdown: Confronting Modern America in the Western Film* (Urbana: University of Illinois Press, 1980), p. 176. Lenihan is one of the first scholars to recognize the critical symbiosis between a successful entertainment genre and the politics of its time. Certainly students of war films have noted this linkage, but others have been reluctant. An important addition to this literature is Roland Lacourbe's two-volume study of spy films and their relationships to national and international affairs since the late 1930s; see Roland Lacourbe, *Nazisme et seconde guerre mondiale dans le cinema d'espionnage* (Paris: Editions Henri Veyrier, 1983), and *La guerre froide dans le cinema d'espionnage* (Paris: Editions Henri Veyrier, 1985).

8. Jenni Calder, *There Must Be a Lone Ranger: The American West in Film and in Reality* (New York: Taplinger, 1975), p. 218.

9. John W. Evans, "Modern Man and the Cowboy," *Television Quarterly* 1, no. 2 (May 1962):33.

10. Will Wright, *Six Guns and Society: A Structural Study of the Western* (Berkeley: University of California Press, 1975), pp. 166-68, 182-84.

11. Larry McMurtry, "Cowboys. Movies, Myths, and Cadillacs: Realism in the Western," in *Man and the Movies*, ed. W. R. Robinson (Baton Rouge: University of Louisiana Press, 1967), pp. 46-52.

12. Joe Hyams, *The Life and Times of the Western Movie* (Bromley, England: Columbia Books, 1983), p. 224.

13. Christian Viviani, *Le western* (Paris: Editions Henri Veyrier, 1982), pp. 17, 123.

14. George S. Gallup, ed., *The Gallup Poll: Public Opinion 1935-1971* (New York: Random House, 1972), pp. 1805-06.

15. Ann Golenpaul, ed., *Information Please Almanac 1976* (New York: Dan Golenpaul Associates, 1975), p. 76; Charles S. Aaronson, ed., *International Television Almanac 1962* (New York: Quigley Publications, 1961), pp. 9A, 22A-26A.

16. J. Fred MacDonald, *Television and the Red Menace: The Video Road to Vietnam* (New York: Praeger, 1985), pp. 148, 205, 247.

17. Richard E. Peck, "Films, Television, and Tennis," in Robinson, *Man and the Movies*, p. 97.

2
The Age of the B Western

The Western found its niche early in the history of television. In fact, among the first popular cultural heroes created by the new electronic medium were the stars of "shoot 'em up" programs. They fought, sang, and romanced their way across countless tiny TV screens; but above all these cowboy stalwarts captured the imagination of a nation of neophyte TV viewers. While their adventures concerned the winning of the West and assuring that justice would prevail, they also won significant victories by drawing audiences to the infant entertainment medium and insuring that television would be a financial and cultural success.

B WESTERN FILMS AND EARLY TV

The original cowboy heroes of TV galloped out of the popular cultural past. They were the sagebrush champions of vintage B Western feature films. This was an improbable development since the bulk of these low-budget movies had been made for theatrical distribution in the 1930s. By the time they came to video in the late 1940s and early 1950s, many of their cowboy stars were middle-aged, retired, or deceased.

The B Western—sometimes called budget Western, or in the words of film historians George N. Fenin and William K. Everson, the "small-scale horse opera"[1] —emerged and flourished during the Depression. Such films were inexpensive to produce and needed only a small box-office draw to be profitable. Furthermore, they had a loyal moviegoing constituency, as they were especially popular with youngsters, rural audiences, and blacks.

The films had simple, formulaic plots; but they were enjoyable for their emphasis on action and their moralistic reiteration of Good victorious over Evil. Although several movie studies continued to make B Westerns until the mid-1950s, the Golden Age for this film style ended during World War II when production costs rose, a new sense of critical realism entered the American cinema, and TV emerged as a competitor.

Nonetheless, the new television industry that emerged in the late 1940s revived many B Western heroes. Names like Tim McCoy, Ken and Kermit Maynard, Wild Bill Elliott, Hoot Gibson, Charles Starrett as the Durango Kid, Tom Mix, and Bob Steele—well respected by children growing up a generation earlier—became household terms again. In fact, the exploits of these sagebrush stars were among the most popular offerings of early TV. By airing their old films, television gave a new set of youngsters those action-filled stories of bold, if somewhat one-dimensional, champions who upheld law and order against an army of assorted outlaws.

The many fistfights, shoot-outs, and chases across the desert underscored the prowess of these revitalized heroes. The various guises in which they encountered evil—cattle rustling, bank robbing, claim jumping, the burning of farms, cold-blooded murder, and the like—only demonstrated their crime-busting versatility. The requisite happy ending that followed their victories stressed the satisfaction inherent in the defeat of immorality by morality.

In those first years of commercial television, Westerns played a key role in generating mass enthusiasm for the medium, especially among children. This was noticeable in the hours when such programs were scheduled. Weekends in the morning and afternoon and weekdays in the late afternoon were filled with cowboy dramatics. Sponsored by bread companies, breakfast cereal manufacturers, bubble gum makers, and similar youth accounts, two-fisted cowboy dramatics permeated juvenile viewing hours.

The verve with which such video approached young people was epitomized in promotional advertisements of the time. One Chicago TV log publicized a program in 1948 by proclaiming, "Cowboys and Indians go rootin' tootin' over the plains, and Tom Mix arrives on Tony in the nick of time to keep a new generation of youngsters from falling off the edge of their seats." A year later the arrival of *The Lone Ranger* on television was heralded: "Yes, now you can SEE the Lone

Ranger and his great horse Silver as he fights for justice and fair play in the sagebrush country." *Hopalong Cassidy* in late 1949 was promoted as

- Thrills . . . Excitement . . . Suspense
- Spine-tingling episodes never shown before on TV
- Hard shootin' . . . hard ridin' sagas of the Old West.[2]

For their part, children in these vintage years of TV strongly supported Western programming. A survey of youngsters in metropolitan New York City in April 1949 determined that cowboy dramas were the favorite entertainment of juvenile viewers. Asked to choose three programs or types of entertainment they most preferred, their tastes emerged as shown in Table 2.

Importantly, too, the popularity of Westerns was high in all age categories as the genre ranked first with children 9 and 10, and second with those 5 to 8 and 11 to 14. Even mothers and fathers seemed to approve, for Westerns ranked second only to Milton Berle's *Texaco Star Theater* as TV fare viewed together by parents and children.

Surveys throughout the early 1950s reaffirmed the popularity of television Westerns. Where adults in early 1950 rated Western features as their eighth-favored type of programming, youths made such offerings their first choice by a wide margin over animated cartoons, comedy shorts, and sports.[3] By April 1951 Westerns were viewed at least once each week by 66.3 percent of homes with children, and by 39.2 percent of those without children.[4] As late as December 1955 such popularity continued as 58.3 percent of those responding admitted

Table 2 Children's Programs, April 1949

First Preference by Program/Type (in percents)

1. Westerns	53.3
2. Howdy Doody	51.1
3. Milton Berle	43.8
4. Lucky Pup	31.4
5. Small Fry Club	30.7
6. Kukla, Fran, and Ollie	27.0

Source: "Study of Children's Programs," *The Television Audience of Today* 1, no. 2 (April 1949). NBC Records, box 193, folder 2. Respondents were allowed three first choice selections.

watching cowboy feature films on TV—and 60.5 percent of these viewers considered such motion pictures to be "as good as, or better than other types of TV movies."[5]

The early match between B Western films and television was a marriage of convenience. With a lack of packaged productions, and the reluctance of the major studios to release their movies for telecasting, the availability of old cowboy features and serials was welcomed by TV. For the companies that produced these films—Mascot, Monogram, PRC, Lone Star, Republic, Columbia, and others—it was also a profitable development. By leasing their old productions to TV they gained unexpected revenue from motion pictures that were anachronisms in most postwar theaters.

In the long run, however, video profited more from the B Westerns. With these movies TV stations were able to expand their hours on the air and, subsequently, sell more time to sponsors. Further, the popularity of the genre enticed hesitant consumers still not persuaded that TV programming was worth the price of a television set.

Countless formulaic features and serials were aired in those premier years of popular TV. A viewer might encounter such stars and titles as Ken Maynard in *Tombstone Canyon* (1932), *Smoking Guns* (1934), *Six Shootin' Sheriff* (1938), or *Western Courage* (1935). Bob Steele could be seen as a scrappy battler for justice in films such as *The Land of Missing Men* (1930), *Law of the West* (1932), and *The Colorado Kid* (1937). Others likely to be viewed included Hoot Gibson in *The Gay Buckaroo* (1932) and *The Riding Avenger* (1936), John Wayne in *Randy Rides Alone* (1934), Tex Ritter in *Hittin' the Trail* (1937), and Larry "Buster" Crabbe in *Billy the Kid in Texas* (1940).

In the heyday of the theatrical B Westerns, the studios churning out this type of entertainment frequently teamed their leading men in series of cowboy movies. Now in early television these ensembles of frontier champions—with names like the Range Busters, Range Riders, Texas Rangers, Rough Riders, Three Mesquiteers, and Trailblazers—were part of the renaissance. Since such filmic teams often included prominent box-office stars—John Wayne and Duncan Renaldo appeared as members of the Three Mesquiteers, Ray "Crash" Corrigan was one of the Range Busters, and Tex Ritter starred in the Texas Ranger series—their corporate pacification of the West complemented their single-handed exploits in other films.

B Westerns were usually telecast locally where they were adapted to nonnetwork demands for time and advertising. They were aired within a showcase called something such as *Six-Gun Playhouse, Sage-brush Theater, Trail Blazers' Theater,* or *Saddle and Sage Theater.* With less imagination, it might be labeled simply *Western Theater* or *Cowboy Playhouse.* Here, the presentation was usually hosted by local personalities dressed in cowboy clothing and named Foreman Tom, Wrangler Bruce, Cactus Jim, Ranger Joe, the Masked Rider, and the like. In several instances, however, celebrities such as Tim McCoy and Iron Eyes Cody in Los Angeles, Buster Crabbe in New York City, and country-western singers Bob Atcher in Chicago and Doye O'Dell in Los Angeles hosted local B Western showcases. Moreover, several such programs even became national offerings: *The Ghost Rider* originated from Philadelphia in 1951-52, but was seen nationally on CBS stations; and in the fall of 1950 Western star Rex Bell hosted *Cowboys 'n' Injuns* in Los Angeles for ABC.

Network interest in the juvenile Western even led to attempts at cowboy series telecast live from TV studios and film lots. *The Marshal of Gunsight Pass* in 1950 starred Russell Hayden and later Eddie Dean in a weekly struggle against desperadoes. It originated from a sound stage of the Vitagraph Studios that ABC had remodeled as its Los Angeles video facility. More ambitious was *Action in the Afternoon,* a serialized midafternoon drama seen weekdays on CBS between February 1953 and January 1954. Set in a Montana town in the 1890s, it originated from suburban Philadelphia and exploited a backlot Western town as well as an indoor studio to relate its tales of the Old West.

As for Western movies, they could be shown in their entirety, edited for commercials and dropped into specified time slots, or segmented and continued over two or more days. Early in the history of TV, local programmers were learning the adaptability of motion pictures to the needs of advertisers.

While feature films required editing to be used as segmented programming, vintage Western serials were tailor-made for this purpose. To tell its entire story each serial usually lasted 12 to 15 separate installments. Since each chapter ran about 12 minutes, serials fit comfortably into quarter-hour or half-hour time periods, still allowing ample time for commercials.

On television, moreover, the cliff-hanger endings, which brought patrons back to movie theaters for each new chapter, now proved equally alluring for TV viewers seeking to know if the hero survived apparent death. Among the more popular Western serials to air in early video was *Custer's Last Stand,* a production from 1936 that offered Rex Lease in a 15-chapter trek toward the Little Big Horn. Also telecast many times locally were Harry Carey in *The Last of the Mohicans* (1932), Tom Mix in *The Miracle Rider* (1935), and the team of Rin-Tin-Tin, Jr. and Rex, "King of the Wild Horses," in *The Law of the Wild* (1934).

THE HOPALONG CASSIDY PHENOMENON

Although the supply of cowboy stalwarts and B films was plentiful, there were few attempts to gather the features of one personality and market him and his movies as a TV series. Syndicated in 1953, *Renfrew of the Royal Mounted* used edited movies from the late 1930s to tell of a Mountie operating in the Canadian West. The quarter-hour *Tim McCoy Show* was an unsuccessful syndicated series in 1955, blending Indian lore and stories of frontier life, all revolving about the old cowboy star and his Cherokee cohost, Iron Eyes Cody. *Saturday Roundup*, an NBC effort featuring Kermit Maynard and his B Westerns, failed to generate enthusiasm when it was broadcast in the early evening in mid-1951. With *Cowboy Theater* NBC returned to this format in 1956-57, now with Monty Hall—later the host of the audience participation show *Let's Make a Deal*—and then cowboy actor Tom Keene hosting on Saturday mornings the B Westerns of Charles Starrett.

Another film notable who failed in this type of TV venture was Lash La Rue whose weekly 15-minute series, *Lash of the West*, had a short run on ABC in 1953. Appearing as the marshal of Sandstone the contemporary Lash La Rue told stories—accomplished through highly edited La Rue Westerns from the late 1940s—of his grandfather of the same name who helped settle the unruly West in the days of the California gold rush.

The program was a classic juvenile offering. Its opening showed La Rue with his smoking six-gun, galloping to rescue a stagecoach under attack by robbers while an energetic announcer proclaimed the array of crimes against which this dynamic hero was effective:

> Daring robberies, rustling, reckless gun duels, range wars, wanton murder, and violence of every kind! But close on the spurred heels of the swaggering outlaws comes Lash La Rue, riding in again with another action-packed saga of the bygone West.

As a quarter-hour, serialized story aired only once a week, *Lash of the West* lacked the visibility necessary to make it a successful TV series. As a Wild West champion dressed in black and relying primarily on his bullwhip to bring justice to the frontier, La Rue lacked the style, charisma, and credibility necessary for popularity.

Where the marketing of Lash La Rue films failed dismally, *The Gabby Hayes Show* lasted considerably longer. For three years in the early 1950s it was a 15-minute program that in late weekday afternoons preceded *Howdy Doody*, a children's program itself starring two cowboy types—"Buffalo Bob" Smith dressed in fringed leather, and the puppet Howdy Doody in blue jeans and gingham shirt. Less impressively, in the summer of 1956 Gabby Hayes appeared on ABC in a Saturday morning half-hour show. In both cases, however, *The Gabby Hayes Show* utilized Western serials and abridged B features of stars like Tex Ritter, Lash La Rue, Buster Crabbe, and Eddie Dean; but the strength of the program was Gabby's distinctive telling of tall tales. In preposterous stories reminiscent of Paul Bunyan and Pecos Bill, he prevaricated on topics such as "how Uncle Weeping Willie created the Pacific Ocean," "how Uncle Welcome Hayes created the first picnic," and "how Aunt Petunia Hayes caused the San Francisco earthquake."

Gabby Hayes notwithstanding, the most successful packaging of a vintage B Western star and his films occurred with the motion pictures of William Boyd. Significantly, this produced the most successful hero of early television: Hopalong Cassidy. Boyd had begun his portrayal of Hopalong Cassidy in 1935. Playing in budget Westerns was a significant change for an actor who had emerged in silent films as a romantic leading man, and who at the outset of his cowboy career was unable to ride a horse.

Yet before he ceased making "Hoppy" motion pictures in 1948, Boyd had mastered horsemanship, completed 66 features, and left a legacy as one of the most popular cowboy stars in the nation. More importantly, as a businessman anticipating the needs of the new visual medium, by 1948 Boyd had gained TV rights to his B Western features as well as the option to produce more Hoppy films expressly for television.

Beginning locally in New York City and Los Angeles, and spreading by 1949 to NBC and national exposure, Hopalong Cassidy experienced phenomenal acceptance. Although the old features were edited to allow for commercials within a one-hour time slot, fans seemed undaunted in their approval of this first video hero. For a 16-month period the program averaged a rating of 32.6, reaching over 4 million homes per weekly telecast.[6] According to the Nielsen ratings for September 1949, *Hopalong Cassidy* was the seventh most popular program—ranked ahead of Jack Carter's *Cavalcade of Stars*, Ted Mack's *Original Amateur Hour*, and *Arthur Godfrey and His Friends*. For the entire 1950-51 TV season, moreover, *Hopalong Cassidy* was ranked ninth—more popular that year than the family-oriented comedy *Mama* (10th), Ed Sullivan's *The Toast of the Town* (15th), Groucho Marx's *You Bet Your Life* (17th), the big-money giveaway feature, *Stop the Music!* (23rd), and such venerable showcases of live drama as *Kraft Television Theater* (14th), *Robert Montgomery Presents* (11th), *Armstrong Circle Theater* (19th), and *Studio One* (24th).

In a pattern followed by other celebrities in the future, television success allowed William Boyd to market his endorsement as Hopalong Cassidy to a wide spectrum of peripheral products. Hoppy roller skates, wastebaskets, lamps, soap, and wristwatches were typical commodities sold with his name and likeness. One million Hopalong Cassidy jackknives were sold in the first ten days of their availability. Hoppy, who usually appeared dressed in black Western clothing, even sold black shirts to children—a singular marketing achievement since in American culture black was associated with mourning or Italian Fascism.

By 1950 William Boyd was riding the crest of a Hopalong Cassidy industry conservatively estimated to be worth $200 million. His films were on 57 TV stations; his new half-hour radio drama was syndicated to 517 outlets; and he appeared in a comic strip reaching 11.2 million readers through 72 daily and 40 Sunday newspapers.[7] Boyd cemented his marketing appeal through his Hopalong Cassidy Troopers Club, a nationally organized promotional arrangement that provided its juvenile members a membership card, secret code, and the *Troopers News*, a four-page periodical paid for by regional sponsors of his TV programs.

The strength of this commercial empire, however, rested with the character Hopalong Cassidy and the values he personified on the TV screen. Astride his pure white horse, Topper, Cassidy was a puritanical figure whose crusade for justice was always accomplished with understated flair. Hoppy never smoked or chewed tobacco. When he entered a saloon he avoided alcohol and usually ordered sarsaparilla. When he spoke with his guns drawn on a desperado, he was grammatically efficient. "Drop them guns on the ground unless you're gonna use 'em," and "Alright, Johnny, tie 'em up. They're through for the day" were authoritative and typically terse orders from Hopalong Cassidy.

While he generally operated with two vulnerable partners—usually a wizened old man played by Gabby Hayes, Andy Clyde, or Edgar

Buchanan, plus a handsome young swain such as Jimmy Ellison, Russell Hayden, or Rand Brooks with whom ranchers' daughters invariably fell in love—Hoppy was all business. No woman ever won his heart. In fact, in all his films Cassidy kissed a woman only once, and she was on her deathbed at the time.

William Boyd understood the impact his portrayal had on viewers. He was especially sensitive to his effect on children. "Hopalong is a simple man, friendly and informal," Boyd remarked in 1950. "He's very intimate. I don't treat kids as kids—they don't like that—I play to the adults. That pleases everybody."[8] Three years earlier he was even more specific in explaining the social direction of his Hoppy movies:

> Then there was the idea that maybe Westerns, which kids have always loved, might be used to teach them things like fair play and having respect for themselves and one another. I even had a hunch that if I could make the right sort of Westerns, never forgetting they had to be action pictures and good entertainment, I might even do my bit to reduce crime among kids and juvenile delinquents.[9]

As a moral force, Hoppy's "hunch" was never more obvious than in the eight-point creed to which a youngster was asked to swear allegiance when accepting membership in the Troopers Club.

> To be kind to birds and animals
> To always be truthful and fair
> To keep yourself neat and clean
> To always be courteous
> To be careful when crossing streets
> To avoid bad habits
> To study and learn your lessons
> To obey your parents

Certainly, Hopalong Cassidy was a commercial enterprise concerned about ratings, residuals, advertising rates, viewer demographics, and profits. Yet, while it was a carefully marketed enterprise, the Cassidy product had broader significance. As with most popular cultural phenomena, Hoppy embodied strategic, relevant social issues. His character and its traits communicated more than a simple story of cowboys versus outlaws.

For a generation of children, many of them born in the deprivation of the Depression or World War II, many having experienced the temporary or permanent loss of a father, the paternal guidance offered by the successful Hopalong was crucial. Cassidy embodied discipline, devotion to others, bravery, and similar values. He completed tasks successfully. He was strong, but always compassionate—a warrior who at heart wanted only social harmony.

Further, in a time of Cold War tensions with atomic-bomb potentialities, Hoppy was a patriot. He loved America with its open frontiers where honest folks settled to raise decent families. He fought for their rights, risking his own life so that the meek could inherit their earth and thrive in the North American wilderness.

Hoppy operated in a black-and-white moral world: One was either good or bad, and Cassidy was uncompromising with those who were bad. His was not a questioning or relativistic loyalty to national ideals. He followed the good course; and like a moral force on horseback, he led a generation of youngsters—and often those parents who approvingly watched with their children—toward realization of what the good person or society could be. The innocence fundamental to Cassidy's cultural message was captured decades later in a poem by singer/songwriter Don McLean:

NO MATTER HOW SCARY LIFE GOT I COULD DEPEND ON YOU
YOU HAD THAT EASY SMILE AND WHITE, WAVY HAIR
YOU WERE MY FAVORITE FATHER FIGURE WITH TWO GUNS BLAZING
NOT EVEN VICTOR JORY COULD STAND UP TO THOSE 44-40'S YOU
  PACKED
AND THAT STALLION YOU RODE, I THINK HIS NAME WAS TOPPER
HE WAS SO BEAUTIFUL AND WHITE HE EVEN CAME WHEN YOU WHISTLED
I'VE ALWAYS LIKED BLACK AND I LOVED YOUR CLOTHES
BLACK HAT, BLACK PANTS AND SHIRT
SILVER SPURS AND TWO GUNS IN BLACK HOLSTERS WITH PEARLY
  WHITE HANDLES
BLACK AND WHITE, THAT WAS YOU HOPPY
THE BAD MEN FELL THE GOOD GUYS LIVED ON
THE LADIES TOUCHED YOUR HAND BUT NEVER KISSED
WHENEVER JOHN CARRADINE ASKED A QUESTION YOU'D SAY
"THAT COMES UNDER THE HEADING OF MY BUSINESS"
THEN YOU'D CALL FOR ANOTHER SARSPARILLA
I BELIEVED IN YOU SO MUCH THAT I'D TAKE MY STETSON
OFF AND PUT IT OVER MY HEART WHENEVER ANYBODY DIED
MY HAT'S OFF TO YOU, HOPPY
SAY GOOD-BYE TO ALL THE BOYS AT THE BAR-20
THE BLACK AND WHITE DAYS ARE OVER
SO LONG HOPALONG CASSIDY.

MADE-FOR-TV WESTERNS: THE FIRST GENERATION

The popularity of Hopalong Cassidy films illustrated early that Americans were attracted to programming that spotlighted a single, recurring personality. Rather than purchase legal rights to their old movies and package them for TV, several stars of vintage Westerns began producing original series expressly for television. Beginning in 1949 viewers encountered an array of these new programs that, however, borrowed much of their quality and spirit from B Westerns. In many instances, moreover, the new shows also borrowed characters, actors, and production units from those older feature films.

The ethos of matinee idols like Buck Jones, Sunset Carson, Whip Wilson, George Houston, and Johnny Mack Brown was found in made-for-TV series such as *The Cisco Kid, The Gene Autry Show, The Lone Ranger, The Adventures of Wild Bill Hickok,* and *The Roy Rogers Show*. Many leading men in these series were already familiar to movie-going youngsters. For more than a decade Gene Autry and Roy Rogers were respected stars of Westerns made at Republic Pictures. They were also popular recording artists, and their radio programs had been network features throughout the 1940s.

While the Cisco Kid and the Lone Ranger had appeared in feature films and serials, they were most familiar as heroes of radio series. In particular, the Lone Ranger had a rich broadcasting career, appearing since 1933 in complete half-hour dramas three times each week.

To write, direct, and photograph the new TV programs, producers were heavily reliant upon personnel with experience in making B Westerns. According to the principal historian of the B Western film, Don Miller, "instead of inventing new techniques of its own, [television] was content to borrow from the established, conventional motion pictures methods."[10]

The Cisco Kid was often directed by Lambert Hillyer, a director of Westerns since the 1920s whose theatrical films featured the likes of William S. Hart, Tim McCoy, Charles Starrett, Wild Bill Elliott, Duncan Renaldo, Johnny Mack Brown, Whip Wilson, Jimmy Wakely, and Buck Jones. Gene Autry formed Flying "A" Productions to create his own program as well as *Annie Oakley, The Range Rider, Buffalo Bill, Jr.,* and a series featuring his celebrated horse, *The Adventures of Champion*. To direct episodes in these series, Autry frequently employed George Archainbaud, a man who at United Artists had directed B Westerns starring William Boyd and Johnny Mack Brown.

The qualities of the B Western permeated *The Adventures of Wild Bill Hickok*. The series was filmed by units experienced in making inexpensive cowboy dramas for Monogram Pictures. True to the tradition of budget features, *Wild Bill Hickok* episodes were produced at a cost of $12,000 each. According to Guy Madison, who portrayed Hickok, "we couldn't waste any time in TV. We made a half-hour show in two-and-a-half days. That included dialogue, action, and everything. At one point we knocked off seven films in seventeen days."[1]

B Western stars appeared in early cowboy TV programs. Russell Hayden, who until 1941 played Hopalong Cassidy's handsome sidekick, Lucky Jenkins, developed and starred in several such series. As early as March 1950 he was featured on ABC in *The Marshal of Gunsight Pass*. Hayden was more successful in *Cowboy G-Men* as well as *Judge Roy Bean*, where he was producer and a star. He later produced *26 Men*—a series depicting the Arizona Rangers at the turn of the century—in which the leading role was played by Tris Coffin, a frequent villain in B features and serials in the 1940s.

Rex Allen, a star of B Westerns in the early 1950s, appeared in 1958 as a physician to the pioneers in *Frontier Doctor*. Even William Boyd responded to the call for TV films. He returned to the saddle to make 52 new Hoppy half-hour programs in 1951-52.

Made-for-TV Westerns were crafted specifically with children in mind. Gene Autry, for example, explained his decision to enter the new medium as an attempt to reach youngsters. "Television had begun to seduce the whole country, and some of us saw it coming earlier than others," wrote Autry in his autobiography. "Around 1950, my company, Flying 'A' Productions, began developing ideas aimed at the kids' market."[2]

George W. Trendle, producer of the radio and video versions of *The Lone Ranger*, explained in 1950 how his series sought to gratify "the hunger for adventure" in children by providing "wholesome devices instead of violence and nightmare-inducing episodes." In summarizing the standards he demanded in the program, Trendle in essence delineated all youth-oriented Westerns popular in early TV. According to him, proper guidelines called for

> making the hero the embodiment of all that is morally desirable; providing the script with the absolute minimum of violence; completing each episode in a single broadcast; basing the plots on events that are not immediately referrable to the child's framework of experience; avoiding "false cliff-hanger" suspense points contrived to appear before the middle commercial to sustain a child's continuing interest; interspersing educational data with adventure.[3]

The central characters in these series were flawless types who blended strength and savvy to overcome injustice. They exhibited no personal vices; they were always gallant around women; and they were never tempted by money to stray from their sanctimonious paths. Many were handsome heroes like Guy Madison in *The Adventures of Wild Bill Hickok*, Bill Williams in *The Adventures of Kit Carson*, and Duncan Renaldo in *The Cisco Kid*. Others emphasized special talents. Gene Autry could sing as well as shoot and ride; Jock Mahoney demonstrated his athletic prowess in *The Range Rider*; and in *Annie Oakley* Gail Davis evidenced pioneering courage as the first and only woman star of her own TV Western.

The heroes and heroine of the genre were emulable stereotypes for American children. They were idealized parents, the perfect big brother or sister, personalities after whom to shape one's emerging adulthood. Here were self-confidence and moderation in adult action. Here, too, were paradigms of dedication to purpose, responsibility to civilized standards, and concern for one's fellow man.

Cognizant of their influence on juvenile viewers, these video characters offered moral guidelines—but not always in the same style. George W. Trendle made his hero thoroughly good, as he instructed his writers to portray the Lone Ranger as a patriotic, God-fearing, tolerant, habitless character who always used good grammar, never shot to kill, and who could "fight great odds, yet take time to treat a bird with a broken wing."[14]

Roy Rogers allowed for more violence in his Western morality plays, justifying such mayhem with reference to history. He once explained that "the Westerns I make come right out of the history books. In those old days, pioneers packed a six-shooter whether they were ploughing or riding herd." In his view of the Old West, the frontiersmen "were blazing new trails, pioneering in new territory, and [they] didn't let any gang of outlaws or ambushing Indians get the drop on them." Within this historical framework Rogers felt violence to be a function of accuracy. "We only fire our guns when necessary. But," he continued, "there's an evil force that always is challenging. And when that challenge comes you have to meet it with spirit and fire."[15]

That Roy Rogers translated this understanding of violence into his TV Westerns was evident to newspaper critic Jack Mabley. Writing in the Chicago *Daily News* after viewing an episode of *The Roy Rogers Show*, he maintained that "it's frightening to see five- and six-year old tots sitting spellbound before TV sets soaking up this sadism." Mabley complained that in the episode he saw, two men beat an old man. . . . the old man is permanently blinded by the attack. Two men beat a dog [Bullet] about the head with a pistol. . . . The men again attack the dog as he is leading the old man on a mountain trail. The old man cries for help, plunges over a cliff to his death. . . . A veterinarian who is a thief kills an injured companion with an injection of poison. . . . The dog is doped but attacks a man. Two men kidnap a girl, then beat her.[16]

Most specific in his moral prescription for the B Western was Gene Autry. In the Cowboy Code he promulgated in the early 1950s, Autry defined ethical, social, and political qualities with which he urged the movie industry to imbue all B Western characterizations. However, Autry intended his guidelines not only for celluloid cowboy heroes, but also for the young fans of the Western. The Code was essentially a secular Ten Commandments with direct application to children in the TV audience.

1. A cowboy never takes unfair advantage, even of an enemy.
2. A cowboy never betrays a trust.
3. A cowboy always tells the truth.
4. A cowboy is kind to small children, to old folks, and to animals.
5. A cowboy is free from racial and religious prejudice.
6. A cowboy is always helpful, and when anyone's in trouble, he lends a hand.
7. A cowboy is a good worker.
8. A cowboy is clean about his person, and in thought, word, and deed.
9. A cowboy respects womanhood, his parents, and the laws of his country.
10. A cowboy is a patriot.[17]

Gene Autry had critics, but to those "sophisticated people" who felt that with his commandments "the cowboy became a sort of adult boy scout," Autry was unbending. He wrote in his autobiography in 1978: "I didn't exactly move in sophisticated circles. I never felt there was anything wrong with striving to be better than you are."[18]

Importantly, Autry's decalogue was relevant not only to the juvenile Western. While theatrical realization may have been predictably unsophisticated in the juvenile Western, and relatively complex in the adult variety that soon prevailed on TV, both formats—indeed all Western dramas in all media—ultimately spoke to the values enunciated in the Cowboy Code. This was well understood by the British scholar, Jenni Calder, when she wrote:

The strength of the Western is that traditionally it has been able to combine the essence of Gene Autry's code with the excitement of human brutality. This is not something new. Legend from time immemorial has been based on just such a fusion. If the Greek heroes are not much concerned with being polite to each other they are always testing themselves against a demanding and ennobling code. The roundtable knights also, and here courtesy and honour are of intrinsic value. Robin Hood and the great legendary bandits have obviously found their way into the Western, and in their case the fundamental decency, the protection of women and the poor, is central. The Western hero belongs solidly with all of these and in spite of changes he will continue to do so.[19]

The stalwarts of juvenile Westerns were dedicated upholders of law and order, defenders of that civility nurtured on the historic American frontier. They were individuals willing to risk everything to guarantee the well-being of average folks. Sometimes they were government agents such as U.S. Army scout Kit Carson or U.S. Marshal Wild Bill Hickok. More often, they were from the common cloth of society, citizen do-gooders like the wandering Lone Ranger and Tonto, or ranchers Sky King, Roy Rogers, and Annie Oakley. Whatever their occupations, theirs were tales of the selfless enforcement of fair laws for fair people.

That laws were crucial for the survival of their frontier civilizations was well understood by the altruistic heroes of television Westerns. In "The Kid from Red Butte," an episode of *The Adventures of Wild Bill Hickok*, Jingles and Wild Bill lectured the misguided son of an outlaw on the meaning of obedience to the law. To the boy's smug remark, "Too bad you're lawmen," Jingles replied ungrammatically, "Well, if there wasn't lawmen the whole West would be completely wild." And Hickok added, "There'd be no decent towns, no churches, no schools."

Focusing more specifically on the personal sacrifices made by Western lawmen, the avuncular Judge Ben Wiley rebuked a skeptic in "The Assassins," an episode in 1956 of *Buffalo Bill, Jr.*

> You listen to me, mister. I've got something to say to you, and you listen. Talkin's easy, but it don't get a lawman very far. He knows a time and a place'll come when he'll have to face guns and fight back. He knows that when he pins on his badge. And you know who he's doin' it for? For you, mister, and me and any other citizen. The pay's no good. The hours are long. But it's his job, and he does it the best he knows how.

Lest these champions appear too invulnerable, most were accompanied around the Wild West by a partner who added human frailty to the show. Opposite the lithe physique of Guy Madison, for example, Andy Devine as Jingles P. Jones was a grossly overweight caricature of the cowboy hero. Jingles was a buckskin buffoon weighing more than 300 pounds whose antics brought more laughs than justice to the wilderness. Jingles once pulled a rabbit out of the back of his buckskin jacket. He ran from homely women who sought him as a possible husband. In fistfights he usually won by bumping opponents with his prodigious belly. Humor emanated particularly from his high-pitched, breaking voice as he interjected such expletives as "great jumpin' horned toads," or when he explained a last-second escape from death: "We were so close to the Pearly Gates we could hear old Gabriel tuning up."

Most of these sidekicks were comics. Pat Brady in *The Roy Rogers Show* was a frenetic type whose confused escapades in a Jeep named Nellybelle added light relief to somber Rogers and serious Dale Evans on horseback. On the syndicated series. *Steve Donovan, Western Marshal*, Rusty Lee was a bewhiskered and amusingly loquacious deputy to the forthright Donovan. On *The Gene Autry Show*, Pat Buttram operated as a bumpkin comedian whose exclamations and puns frequently lacked imagination. He could mumble something as silly as "I'll be diddly dad-burned"; or while conducting business in a bank, he could joke that bank tellers "are nice people because they will tell you anything you want to hear."

In Pancho, the friend of the Cisco Kid, actor Leo Carrillo added minstrel-show ethnic stereotyping to the comedic Western partnership. Pancho spoke with an exaggerated Mexican accent peppered liberally with malaprops. He loved to eat and was, understandably, a paunchy comrade of the agile Cisco.

Nevertheless, Pancho possessed the human frailty and emotionality absent in his one-dimensional partner. Pancho could express confusion, as when approached by men with drawn pistols he once remarked, "What is this, Cisco—good men who think we are bad, or bad men who think we are good?" More simply, he could moan, "I get all mixed up in my brains." Pancho could be rascalish and misinform a spinster with designs on Cisco that his partner was actually married and the father of seven children. As never evidenced in a hero, Pancho could also show fear and cowardice, as in the following exchange from "Romany Caravan," an episode from January 1951.

Cisco: I'm ashamed of you, Pancho, running away from a bear.
Pancho: Yeah, but Cisco, I, eh, eh—
Cisco: Come on, we're going right back.
Pancho: But, Cisco, that bear, h-h-h-he's got a hungry look in his
         eyes.
Cisco: Say, what are you, a man or a mouse?
Pancho: Right now, I'm a little mousie.
Cisco: If that's the way you feel about it, here's where we part
         company.
Pancho: Oh, Cisco, don't leave me, don't leave me alone here with
         a, Cisco, don't leave me alone here with a . . .

Of course, the function of a sidekick was not always linked to comic relief. Even Pancho and Jingles could use guns and fists in assisting their brave pals. In several series, moreover, the partner was clearly not a comedian. Dick West was a romantic, even "all-American boy" type when he traveled with the Range Rider. Annie Oakley was assisted on occasion by her kid brother, Tagg, as well as by Lofty Craig, the handsome town sheriff. *The Adventures of Kit Carson* featured El Toro, a Mexican-accented partner whose humorous side was usually subordinated to amorous flirtations and the physical demands of bringing social stability to frontier California.

In Tonto, the Indian assistant of the Lone Ranger, the relationship between juvenile hero and sidekick was its most sophisticated. Tonto was never clownish, nor was he less courageous than his "kemo sabe." The only impediments to his full equality with the Ranger were his constant use of pidgin English and the fact that he encountered racial prejudice in white society. Yet Tonto possessed physical strength, intellectual ability, and moral integrity. He never failed to merit the trust placed in him by the Lone Ranger and by viewers. On many occasions, too, Tonto's actions saved the life of his partner. More than a friendship, the bond between Tonto and the Ranger was an alliance between mature men who recognized their interdependency and innate equality.

Importantly, too, Tonto was an assimilated Indian, a partner who embraced the white man's dominion and now rode to enforce its laws. As historian Ralph Brauer has pointed out, in programs dealing with Indian unrest *The Lone Ranger* stressed that there were good Indians like Tonto and bad Indians like those unwilling to accept and adapt to the Westward movement of the settlers from the East. Tellingly, the episode entitled "The Courage of Tonto," aired January 17, 1957, began with an announcer proclaiming: "The Apaches fought long and hard to stem the tide of civilization."[20] Indeed in Tonto—the generic Indian whose tribal affiliation was unstated and unimportant—there was none of this Apachelike "uncivilized" intransigence. Tonto was the "new Indian": a representation of political, cultural, and intellectual acceptance of white civilization by the aboriginal population.

Whatever the role, gallant hero or comedic subaltern, characterization in these early Westerns was fundamentally unbelievable. From Gene Autry's singing, to Jingles P. Jones obesity, to Sky King's Cessna P-50 and later P-130 airplanes, these were not the guises of the actual men and women who settled and maintained the West.

In the cases of *The Roy Rogers Show* and *Annie Oakley*, moreover, entire series were constructed upon such incredibility. Brave Roy operated in a classic Western locale—Mineral City situated in Paradise Valley—complete with horses, a saloon, and six-guns holstered to the hips of its male citizens. Yet Roy's partner, Pat Brady, drove a Jeep of post-World War II vintage. Although a gasoline station was never shown, Mineral City did have telephones. Moreover, Dale Evans added to the anomaly. She appeared at times as a waitress in her own Eureka hotel and cafe, as a gun-toting sharpshooter who rode with Roy to capture outlaws, or as a surrogate mother for the orphaned or otherwise abandoned children written into many *Roy Rogers* episodes. Further, it was well-known that in reality Evans and Rogers were married, but the program never portrayed "the Queen of the West" and "the King of the Cowboys" as anything but mutually supportive friends.

From its action-filled opening credits *Annie Oakley* projected a heroine unprecedented in the video Western. As portrayed by B Western star Gail Davis, Oakley was shown riding at full gallop; then she jumped from horseback to a fast-moving stagecoach; and finally, as her horse sped past a man holding a playing card, she stood straight up in her stirrups and fired a bullet through the center of the nine of spades. Behind this montage of shooting and action scenes, a male announcer energetically proclaimed: "Bull's eye! Annie Oakley hits the entertainment bull's eye every week with her hard ridin', straight shootin', and suspense."

With her two pigtails and white-fringed leather clothing, Oakley did not appear to be the female equivalent of the masculine stalwarts of cowboy law and order; but she wore a gun on her right hip, shot with uncanny accuracy, and was appreciated as a threat to criminal activities. In an episode from 1956 entitled "Dude's Decision," a stage-coach driver succinctly informed a group of outlaws that they should fear the woman riding to his rescue.

Outlaw #1:   Look over there, up on that rise.
Outlaw #2:   Ah, we got company.
Outlaw #3:   Let's get going.
Outlaw #2:   It's only a girl.
    Driver: That's not only a girl, that's Annie Oakley.
Outlaw #3:   Let's move!

Writing in late 1952, Gene Autry revealed his secret for making successful TV Westerns. "Keep it simple, keep it moving, keep it close and make it fast," was his professional advice.[21] Nowhere did he suggest that producers need be concerned with the believability of the stories they were filming. Turning out children's entertainment products did not demand great attention to whether or not the events depicted did or could actually happen.

Typically, such indifference was demonstrated in "Lost Indian Mine," an episode in January 1952 of *The Adventures of Wild Bill Hickok*. Here Hickok and Jingles spent their energies protecting a young boy and his grandfather who, while prospecting in an ancient Aztec cave, were threatened by greedy men anxious to find buried treasure. At the end of the story—after Wild Bill had rescued the innocents from the outlaws—Jingles clumsily threw a stick of dynamite into a kerosene lamp causing an explosion. As the dust settled, Hickok, Jingles, the boy, and his grandfather found themselves covered with pearl necklaces, gold, and other gems. Jingles had accidently unearthed Aztec treasure missing since the time of Cortez. It was a formulaic happy ending to a typically simple story.

For years in literature and motion pictures the Western had been a mature, inventive art form; but in television into the mid-1950s, the genre was unmistakably for children. Critics assailed these TV Westerns as routine. They attacked their plots as "eternally the same, the characters unchanging, the scenery a belt-line panorama of dusty plain, high boulders and an occasional large tree suitable for hanging."[22] Writers, sponsors, advertising agencies, and network officials, all convinced that the genre was juvenile entertainment, were reluctant to consider it anything but an adolescent vehicle, despite the fact that adults also watched these series.

Indicative of this attitude, a report on the TV Western made for NBC in late 1952 drew conclusions relative to the influence of juveniles in the audience:

1. Low income and large family owners are the strongest enthusiasts for such programs;
2. Most of the feeling that Westerns are harmful to children comes from families without children:
   - 74 percent of all families with children said Westerns were alright if not presented too often—only 52 percent of childless families drew this conclusion;
   - 37 percent of parents believed children actually benefitted by watching Westerns; 30 percent believed children were harmed watching Westerns; while 70 percent did not believe children were harmed by watching Westerns;
   - 13 percent of childless families would ban the Western from television; only 5 percent of families with children would agree to such a ban.[23]

Although the video Western continued to be fashioned primarily for youngsters, by the mid-1950s the genre appeared with more sophistication and improved production values. It is possible to distinguish these later programs and limited-run series as a second generation of video cowboy dramas.

MADE-FOR-TV WESTERNS: THE SECOND GENERATION

In the middle of the decade juvenile Westerns gave evidence of new creative energy. At the moment when the earlier series were reaching the end of their original runs, a new generation of children's Westerns entered American video. As Table 3 illustrates, several juvenile Westerns enjoyed lengthy acceptance by viewers.

In production values and story content the second generation of juvenile Westerns was generally more intricate than earlier series. Several were from major motion picture studios. Columbia Pictures, through its TV subsidiary Screen Gems, produced *The Adventures of Rin Tin Tin*; and Walt Disney Productions filmed *Zorro* and several serialized hour-long films appearing on the *Disneyland* program.

In *Brave Eagle* and *Sergeant Preston of the Yukon*, the youth-oriented Western demonstrated a high level of complexity. *Brave Eagle* focused on a young Cherokee chief trying to keep a peaceful balance between evil white men and Indians anxious to answer the white man's bigotry with their tomahawks. The series projected an image of the

Table 3 Juvenile Western Television Series

Name of Program	First-Run Years	Episodes
First Generation, 1948-54		
Hopalong Cassidy	1948-52	66 features
		52 TV films
The Lone Ranger	1949-57	221
The Marshall of Gunsight Pass	1950	*
Cowboys 'n' Injuns	1950-51	*
The Cisco Kid	1950-56	156
The Gene Autry Show	1950-56	86
The Gabby Hayes Show	1950-54	*
	1956	10
Saturday Roundup	1951	12
The Range Rider	1951-52	78
The Ghost Rider	1951-52	*
Sky King	1951-54	130
The Adventures of Kit Carson	1951-55	104
The Roy Rogers Show	1951-57	104
The Adventures of Wild Bill Hickok	1951-58	113
Cowboy G-Men	1952	39
Lash of the West	1952	39
Renfrew of the Royal Mounted	1953	13
Action in the Afternoon	1953-54	*
Annie Oakley	1954-57	81
The Tim McCoy Show	1955	39
Steve Donovan, Western Marshal	1955	39
The Adventures of Champion	1955-56	26
Buffalo Bill, Jr.	1955-56	40
Cowboy Theater	1956-57	39
Second Generation, 1954-59		
Davy Crockett†	1954-55	5
The Adventures of Rin Tin Tin	1954-58	164
Brave Eagle	1955-56	26
Sergeant Preston of the Yukon	1955-58	78
Tales of the Texas Rangers	1955-58	52
Judge Roy Bean	1956	39
Hawkeye and the Last of the Mohicans	1957	39
The Saga of Andy Burnett†	1957-58	6
Zorro	1957-59	78
26 Men	1957-59	78

(Table 3 continues)

Table 3 *(Continued)*

Name of Program	First-Run Years	Episodes
Frontier Doctor	1958	39
The Nine Lives of Elfego Baca[†]	1958-60	10
Tales of Texas John Slaughter[†]	1958-61	17
Zorro[†]	1960-61	4
Daniel Boone[†]	1960-61	4

*Figure not available

[†]Hour-long TV films appearing on *Disneyland*.

Sources: Loretta Hanley, ed., *Series, Serials & Packages. A TV Film/Tape Source Book* (New York: Broadcast Information Bureau, 1974); Larry James Gianakos, ed., *Television Drama Series Programming: A Comprehensive Chronicle, 1947-1982*, 4 vols. (Metuchen, N.J.: Scarecrow Press, 1978-83); Alex McNeil, *Total Television: A Comprehensive Guide to Programming from 1948 to the present* (New York: Penguin Books, 1984); George W. Woolery, *Children's Television: The First Thirty-Five Years, 1946-1981. Part II: Live, Film, and Tape Series* (Metuchen, N.J.: Scarecrow Press, 1985); Don Miller, *Hollywood Corral* (New York: Popular Library, 1976) pp. 241-43; Vincent Terrace, *Encyclopedia of Television Series, Pilots and Specials, 1937-1977*, vol. I (New York: New York Zoetrope, 1986).

American Indian as respectable, a figure whose basic instincts were the protection of home and family and for peace with the white man. Although the star of *Brave Eagle* was not a Native American, the program gained credibility because several of its supporting characters were portrayed by authentic American Indians.

Sergeant Preston of the Yukon concerned a member of the Royal Canadian Mounted Police. Based on a popular radio series, this program offered a Mountie with his husky dog—Yukon King, "the swiftest and strongest lead dog" in the Yukon and Northwest territories—fighting on snowshoes as easily as on horseback to bring social stability to the northwestern Canadian frontier. *Sergeant Preston* emerged from a radio series produced by the same company responsible for *The Lone Ranger*. When translated to television, however, *Sergeant Preston* represented a noticeable maturation in production standards compared to its more famous relative.

The Lone Ranger continually exploited the same sand and boulders of Southern California. Especially after its first season when most of its action was filmed at outdoor locations, the series relied heavily upon less expensive indoor sets and painted backdrops to depict the scenic beauty of the Old West. Such cost-cutting prompted Don Miller to conclude about *The Lone Ranger*: "Except for the two leads, everything about the series smacked of the second rate. Many entire plots were filmed within the confines of a cramped studio set, with outdoor locales ineptly imitated."[24]

In *Sergeant Preston of the Yukon*, however, there was uniqueness. Although its plots perpetuated the simple good-versus-bad predictability of the juvenile TV Western, the series was exceptional in terms of its graphic imagery. Much of its dialogue was shot outdoors. Set as it was in and near the Canadian Arctic, this meant photography uncommon for the genre.

Filmed in the mountains of Colorado and California, here were authentic forests, hills, rivers, and snowscapes. Preston's adventures ranged from grasslands and wooded areas where he operated on his horse, to the frozen wilderness where he maneuvered his dogs and sled. In an episode from 1956 entitled "Dog Race," for example, Preston became involved in a competitive race across deep snows. The program offered scenes of fast-moving sleds and snow storms: here were survival and triumph in the icy primeval. Another episode, "Trouble at Hogback," aired October 13, 1955, placed Sgt. Preston on horseback rising among forests and lakes, while dealing effectively with local Indian and white residents.

Several action series also contributed to the maturation of the TV Western. Ironically, most of these programs—*Frontier Doctor, Hawkeye and the Last of the Mohicans, Judge Roy Bean, 26 Men,* and *Tales of the Texas Rangers*—starred men whose careers were fashioned years earlier in theatrical B Western films. For the most part these shows were syndicated directly to local stations. Only *Tales of the Texas Ranger* had a network history as it appeared for three years on CBS in the late afternoons, and in the early evening on ABC in 1958-59.

Still, with their emphasis upon characterization and on-location photography, these programs helped to attract adults to the audience for TV Westerns. With *Frontier Doctor* Rex Allen portrayed a physician administering to settlers in the Old West. *Hawkeye and the Last of the Mohicans* featured John Hart—who had starred as the Lone Ranger for two TV seasons—and Lon Chaney, Jr. as James Fenimore Cooper's celebrated characters, the eighteenth century backwoodsman, Nat "Hawkeye" Cutler, and his Indian blood brother, Chingachgook. In *Judge Roy Bean* character actor Edgar Buchanan—Hopalong

Cassidy's sidekick in the 52 made-for-TV films produced by William Boyd—turned the historically autocratic Judge Roy Bean into "one man, a storekeeper who was sick of the lawlessness," the hero who brought "civilization and law" west of the Pecos river.

The Arizona Rangers of the early twentieth century were glorified in *26 Men*, a series filmed on location in Tuscon. The stories on *Tales of the Texas Rangers* covered a wide chronological gap, jumping as they did between 1830 and 1950.

The most successful series in this second generation of children's Westerns was more conventional in its setting. *The Adventures of Rin Tin Tin* was an action-filled program spotlighting the alluring combination of a likable boy and his talented German Shepherd dog. Set on a U.S. Cavalry post in the 1880s, *Rin Tin Tin* gave viewers Wild West adventure, avuncular supporting characters—specifically, a handsome lieutenant and a garrulous sergeant—as well as Rusty and "Rinty." It was a popular combination of characters and Western mystique. Even after completing its original production of 164 episodes by 1958, the series was rerun on network TV until the fall of 1964 when it was released to general syndication.

If the juvenile Western enjoyed a new burst of creativity and popularity in the mid-1950s, few contributed more to this renaissance than Walt Disney. When his motion picture company—long famous for its cartoon shorts, animated feature films, and wildlife documentaries—began producing Westerns for television, the result had an overwhelming impact on the medium and the nation.

For two years *Zorro* was an exciting prime-time series. It related romanticized stories of a Mexican nobleman, Don Diego de la Vega, the effete son of a wealthy rancher in Spanish California in the 1820s. Secretly, however, Don Diego was the legendary Zorro, the masked avenger and champion of the downtrodden who consistently outfoxed the tyrannical military authorities. With his black cape flowing, his sword in hand, and atop a surging black stallion, the intrepid Zorro rescued señoritas, defended the abused, and thwarted the designs of villainous men. Adding delicious insult to the injury he inflicted upon the perpetrators of evil, Zorro left his monogram at the scene of all victories, the letter "Z" sliced ever so elegantly with the tip of his rapier. Through 78 half-hour episodes and four hour-long TV movies, this bold renegade brought justice to old California and favorable attention to the Disney studio.

The spirit and execution in *Zorro*, however, still reflected the heritage of B Westerns and the cowboy series of early TV. First, the stories were serialized, telling a complete story in about a dozen episodes, only to segue into another multipart dramatic adventure. Further, the notion of a dual identity and the image of a wealthy but self-sacrificing Robin Hood were not uncommon in Western movies and serials in the 1930s and 1940s.

For efficiency, Don Diego/Zorro had a mute assistant; for laughs he had an imposing comedic foil in the rotund, blundersome, and benign Sergeant Garcia; and for dramatic tension, Zorro had rivals such as the despotic Magistrato Galindo, whose brutal rule weighed heavily upon the common people, and The Eagle, a would-be dictator with designs upon Spanish California.

While Disney gave modern flesh and flair to the suave Zorro, the character was not the creation of his company. He was the literary invention of writer Johnston McCulley who introduced him in a short story, "The Curse of Capistrano," published in 1919 in the pulp magazine *All-Story*. In *The Mark of Zorro* in 1920 and *Don Q, Son of Zorro* in 1925, Douglas Fairbanks, Sr. portrayed the caped avenger in two swashbuckling silent films. Zorro first appeared in talking movies in *The Bold Caballero*, a Republic color feature released in 1937.

There were several other Zorro feature films before Disney brought the character to TV. Perhaps the most celebrated cinematic treatment occurred in 1940 when Tyrone Power appeared in a remake of *The Mark of Zorro*. The romantic Zorro was also the focus of several movie serials from Republic Pictures. These included *Zorro Rides Again* (1937), *Zorro's Fighting Legion* (1939), *Son of Zorro* (1947), and *Ghost of Zorro* (1949). This last serial starred Clayton Moore at the time he was beginning his television portrayal of the Lone Ranger.[25]

THE DAVY CROCKETT PHENOMENON

Even before *Zorro*, however, Disney had demonstrated a mastery of the juvenile Western. His cinematic treatment of the life of Davy Crockett was not properly a television series. It premiered in three separate, hour-long episodes of the *Disneyland* program: *Davy Crockett, Indian Fighter* was telecast on December 15, 1954, as the eighth installment in that influential Disney anthology show; *Davy Crockett Goes to Congress* appeared on January 26, 1955; and the trilogy ended on February 23 with *Davy Crockett at the Alamo*. No program before or since has captured the imagination of the nation in so short a period. Nielsen ratings placed the number of viewers of the second program at more than half of all people watching TV.

Before the finale was aired, the United States was gripped in a Davy Crockett craze.

Davy Crockett hysteria meant an unprecedented commercial boom. Spurred by youngsters and their faddish taste for the TV show, Americans spent upwards of $100 million in Davy Crockettry. More than 4 million copies of the record, "The Ballad of Davy Crockett," were sold; and 14 million Davy Crockett books were purchased.

Since Disney did not have exclusive control of the historic name and likeness of Crockett—as William Boyd and the estate of author Clarence E. Mulford possessed title to everything associated with Hopalong Cassidy—there quickly were an estimated 3,000 different Davy Crockett products for sale. From bath towels and plastic ice cream cones, to ukeleles, underwear, and wristwatches. Davy's name or familiar representation in fringed leather clothing and coonskin cap triggered a consumerist binge.

The fad flourished about seven months, abating only when, as sociologist Paul Lazarsfeld reported at the time, "almost every child has his cap, rifle, powderhorn, book and record."[26] Thus, when *Disneyland* offered two new Crockett TV films in late 1955—*Davy Crockett's Keelboat Race* (November 16), and *Davy Crockett and the River Pirates* (December 14)—millions watched but few were anxious to resume the merchandising mania.

Encouraged by ABC, for the next several years Walt Disney continued to produce Westerns for *Disneyland*. Made-for-TV films featuring heroes like Daniel Boone, Andy Burnett, Texas John Slaughter, Elfego Baca, and Zorro were popular, but they never triggered the social or commercial reaction precipitated by the first Crockett TV movies. Even a repeat of the original trilogy in late 1959 failed to elicit a significant response.

In the history of the video Western the Davy Crockett programs were transitional. Although designed for children, they displayed adult values and relatively mature sensibilities. Certainly, Davy had familiar juvenile embellishments. His partner and pal, Georgie Russell, stayed with him from obscurity in backwoods Tennessee to immortality at the Alamo. His rifle was affectionately named "Old Betsy." Davy operated in a simplified world of black-and-white issues, and he possessed a moral mandate bordering on sacrosanctity.

Crockett also had grown-up qualities. The death of his wife lent bereavement and character-building vulnerability to Davy. He was also a patriot. Davy may have been familiar as a frontiersman in fringed buckskin clothing, but as a political philosopher he was uncommon—

an unreconstructed democrat who was especially outspoken during his short career as a member of the U.S. House of Representatives.

In seeking elective office, he told his friend and fellow Tennessean, President Andrew Jackson, that if elected to Congress, "I wouldn't be takin' orders from you, General. I'd be takin' 'em from them that elected me." In Washington, Davy chided fellow congressmen eager to break treaties and grab valuable Indian land, telling them "Expansion ain't no excuse for persecutin' a whole part of our people because their skins is red and they're uneducated to our ways." With plenty of backwoods allusions, he reminded them—and contemporary Americans as well—that running the nation, indeed even being part of the nation, was serious business. "We got a responsibility to this strappin', fun-lovin', britches-bustin' young b'ar cub of a country," Davy declared with noble innocence, "We've got a responsibility to help it grow into the kinda nation the Good Lord meant it to be."

In his maiden speech to Congress, the unpretentious Crockett explained himself in the rhetoric of the common folk:

> I'm Davy Crockett, fresh from the backwoods. I'm half horse, half alligator, and a little tached with snappin' turtle. I got the fastest horse, the prettiest sister, the surest rifle, and the ugliest dog in Tennessee. My father can lick any man in Kentucky, and I can lick my father. I can hug a bear too close for comfort, and eat any man alive opposed to Andy Jackson. Now, some Congressmen take a lot of pride in sayin' a lot about nothin', like I'm doin' right now. . . . Others don't do nothin' for their pay but just listen day in and day out. I wish I may be shot if I don't do more than listen.

The death and violence depicted in the Davy Crockett movies were also unprecedented in television Westerns. In a genre long used to good, clean fistfights and heroes who shot outlaws only in the hands and arms, there was considerable loss of life in the fictionalized accounts of Crockett's career. There were bloody confrontations with the warring Creek Indians. Shootings, knife fights, and brutal hand-to-hand combat were plentiful. Furthermore, until these programs no TV Western champion had ever died; but at the Alamo, national legends like Colonels Jim Bowie and William B. Travis were slain by Mexican troops, and Davy's life-long sidekick was shot and killed by the besieging enemy. Crockett himself was last seen out of ammunition and swinging his rifle at a swarm of invading Mexican soldiers, about to die in the fight for American territorial expansion.

Long before the so-called adult Western premiered in the fall of 1955, the *Davy Crockett* features illustrated the potential impact of mature Westerns on viewers. Walt Disney later suggested a causal relationship between these films and adult cowboy dramas. As he told an interviewer, "I gave ABC their first full-hour Western series with my Davy Crockett shows and soon the network was flooded with other Westerns."[27]

While Disney may not have been accurate in that assessment of his impact on television—*The Life and Legend of Wyatt Earp* was in production before the Crockett fad swept the nation—the Davy Crockett phenomenon could not have helped but impress TV producers and network executives. Furthermore, if *Davy Crockett* did help spark the revolution in video Westerns, Disney certainly kept the fire alive with his other short frontier series. Featured on *Disneyland* in the years after the Crockett explosion were the limited-run productions *The Saga of Andy Burnett, The Nine Lives of Elfego Baca,* and *Tales of Texas John Slaughter*, as well as *Zorro* and *Daniel Boone.*

Typical of the Disney cowboy hero, John Slaughter was a fast-draw sharpshooter who joined the Texas Rangers to help clear desperadoes from frontier Texas. Elfego Baca was a lawyer—the first Latino lawman in TV history and as deadly with his guns as with his law books—who brought law and order to nineteenth-century New Mexico. Andy Burnett was a frontiersman from Pennsylvania who found most of his adventures struggling against Blackfeet Indians in the Colorado wilderness.

Disney's heroes were streamlined embodiments of American history and morality; but they could be as tough as the worlds in which they operated. Thus, Texas John Slaughter was introduced in each episode as the man "who made 'em do what they ought-er, for if they didn't they died." Baca may have worn a business suit, but he was invincible in a fistfight, and in appropriate situations not averse to killing a foe in a gunfight. Burnett, who was captured by Blackfeet warriors, endured painful ordeals but eventually became an honorary member of the tribe and came to appreciate and participate in Indian ways.

Such representations contained mature qualities not found in early TV Westerns. Disney extracted Andy Burnett from adult-oriented stories written by Stewart Edward White and serialized in *The Saturday Evening Post* in the 1930s. The Burnett films were intended by screenwriter Tom Blackburn as less a Western than "the dramatization of an historical novel. . . . an attempt to recreate honestly the period of the mountain men."[28]

Tales of Texas John Slaughter productions were based on the real-life exploits of an early Texas Ranger. On the premier telecast of the series on October 31, 1958, Walt Disney—described by movie critic and biographer Richard Schickel as "a lonely man in love with vanished graces"[29]—appeared on camera to add humanizing authenticity to his new filmic characterization:

> Well, I have a personal interest in John Slaughter, too. Our research department discovered that when Mrs. Slaughter died in 1942, among her personal affects were 100 shares of Walt Disney Productions stocks. That just goes to show that this old West that we talk about is not so old afterall. It's only yesterday in this young country of ours. Yes, John Slaughter was quite a man.

Although Disney may not have caused the adult Western to appear on TV in the mid-1950s, the commercial and cultural impact of *Davy Crockett*, and the attractive Western characters he developed on *Disneyland*, gave strong support to those who may have decided that the time was propitious to take the video Western out of its adolescence and introduce it as mature drama. The history of the genre during the next decade and a half is testimony to the soundness of such business and cultural decision.

NOTES

1. George N. Fenin and William K. Everson, *The Western from Silents to Cinerama* (New York: Orion Press, 1962), p. 301.

2. *Television Forecast*, August 30, 1948, p. 10; September 24, 1949, p. 13; November 19, 1949, p. 5.

3. "Study of Television Movies," *The Television Audience of Today* 1, no. 11 (January 1950). NBC Records, box 193, folder 8.

4. "Television Western Programs," *The Television Audience of Today* 3, no. 26 (April 1951). NBC Records, box 193, folder 15.

5. "Television Movie Programs," *The Television Audience of Today* 7, no. 82 (December 1955). NBC Records, box 193.

6. *Television*, September 1952, p. 1.

7. *Variety*, May 24, 1950, pp. 2, 18.

8. Oliver Jensen, "Hopalong Hits the Jackpot," *Life*, June 12, 1950, p. 63.

9. Charles Hastings, "The War of the Cowboys," *Motion Picture Magazine*, November 1947, p. 86. For Boyd's views on TV and the family, see *Variety*, December 29, 1954, p. 33.

10. Don Miller, *Hollywood Corral* (New York: Popular Library, 1976), p. 241. For an exhaustive listing of credits for Western feature films, see Les Adams and Buck Rainey, *Shoot-em-Ups: The Complete Reference Guide to Westerns of the Sound Era* (New Rochelle, NY: Arlington House, 1978).

11. Gary H. Grossman, *Saturday Morning TV* (New York: Dell, 1981), p. 170.

12. Gene Autry, *Back in the Saddle Again* (New York: Doubleday, 1978), p. 101.

13. *Variety*, February 8, 1950, p. 32. David Rothel, *Who Was That Masked Man? The Story of the Lone Ranger* (South Brunswick, N.J., A. S. Barnes, 1976), p. 86. David Willson Parker, "A Descriptive Analysis of The Lone Ranger as a Form of Popular Art." Ph.D. dissertation, Northwestern University, 1955, pp. 202-07.

14. *Newsweek*, February 2, 1953, p. 75.

15. Hastings, "The War of the Cowboys," p. 85.

16. Grossman, *Saturday Morning TV*, p. 184n.

17. Gene Autry, "Gene Autry's Prize Round-up," *Radio-Television Mirror*, July 1951, pp. 46, 86. Compare his revised language in Autry, *Back in the Saddle Again*, p. 184. As well as Autry's Cowboy Code and the code of conduct associated with Hopalong Cassidy's Trooper Club, a similar set of moral directives was developed for the short-lived series, *The Ghost Rider*. Here the white-caped host used his Ghost Rider's Club to instill positive social values in the juvenile audience. The Rider pledged viewers to do their homework, cultivate tidy habits, brush their teeth, assist with household chores, help mom each day, and, of course, watch the program. To insure that children followed these few precepts, mothers were encouraged to fill out a daily "good performance" card recording the progress of their youngsters. See George W. Woolery, *Children's Television: The First Thirty-Five Years, 1946-1981. Part II: Live, Film, and Tape Series* (Metuchen, N.J.: Scarecrow Press, 1985), p. 196.

18. Autry, *Back in the Saddle Again*, pp. 184-85.

19. Jenni Calder, *There Must Be a Lone Ranger: The American West in Film and in Reality* (New York: Taplinger, 1975), p. 186.

20. Ralph Brauer, *The Horse, the Gun and the Piece of Property: Changing Images of the TV Western* (Bowling Green, Ohio: Popular Press, 1975), p. 40.

21. Gene Autry, "Producing a Western," *Television Magazine*, October 1952, p. 25.

22. *TV Guide*, September 18, 1953, p. 28.

23. Lawrence C. Ruddick to Thomas E. Coffin, January 15, 1953. NBC Records, box 193, folder 24.

24. Miller, *Hollywood Corral*, p. 242.

25. Alan G. Barbour, *Days of Thrills and Adventure* (New York: Collier Books, 1970), pp. 39-40.

26. Peter T. White, "Ex-King of the Wild Frontier," New York *Times Magazine*, December 11, 1955, p. 27. See also Donald F. Glut and Jim Harmon, *The Great Television Heroes*. (Garden City, N.Y.: Doubleday, 1975), pp. 110-16. For a fuller account of the commercial fad, see Margaret Jane King, "The Davy Crockett Craze: A Case Study in Popular Culture." Ph.D. dissertation, University of Hawaii, 1976.

27. Bill Davidson, "Walt Disney: The Latter-Day Aesop," *TV Guide*, May 20, 1961, p. 27; Leonard Maltin, *The Disney Films* (New York: Crown, 1973), pp. 291-92.

28. " 'The Saga of Andy Burnett'—Davy Crockett Retold?" *TV Guide*, February 22, 1958, p. 6.

29. Richard Schickel, *The Disney Version: The Life, Times, Art, and Commerce of Walt Disney* (New York: Simon and Schuster, 1968), p. 300.

3
The Adult Western: The Flourishing

With the coming of the adult Western, American video audiences experienced a break with the past. While children continued to view this new type of program, here was a prime-time cowboy action designed principally for grown-ups. No longer would the central characters of TV Westerns be those flawlessly moral, one-dimensional types spawned by B film tradition. Brave and tough they would remain, but heroes in the newer series were sketched with more believability and depth of character.

Certainly, there were varieties of adultness in these adult Westerns. Some were more mature than others in terms of characterization and thematic emphasis. Some might even feature youngsters in supporting roles. However, where the juvenile Western stressed the frontier as a theater for two-fisted action, the adult Western envisioned the American wilderness as a stage primarily for the unfolding of human drama.

THE COMPONENTS OF THE ADULT WESTERN

Adult Westerns were recognizable immediately by their sponsors. Where Kellogg's Sugar Pops and General Mills's Cheerios were peddled on *Wild Bill Hickok* and *The Lone Ranger*, respectively, the newer cowboy dramas were now underwritten by expensive, obviously adult products. During the 1959-60 TV season, for example, Greyhound buslines sponsored *Cimarron City* and *Sugarfoot*. For its Wylls Jeep automobiles, Kaiser sponsored *Maverick*, while Buicks were sold on *Tales of Wells Fargo*, Fords on *Dick Powell's Zane Grey Theater*,

Edsels on *Wagon Train*, Gulf gasoline on *The Californians*, Geritol on *The Texan*, Burgermeister beer on *Trackdown*, and Dristan on *Bronco*. For its several brands of cigarettes (L & M, Chesterfield, Duke, Oasis), the Liggett & Myers tobacco company bought commercial time on *Black Saddle, Laramie, The Rebel, Bonanza, Hotel de Paree*, and *Gunsmoke*. For its soap products—from laundry detergents to toothpastes to shampoos—Procter & Gamble advertised on 15 different adult Westerns.

This was a persuasive adult sales alignment. Its effectiveness was best summarized in the flourishing of "the Marlboro man." As a rugged, manly tobacco user—a successful advertising concept from the Leo Burnett agency in 1954—the Marlboro man quickly evolved from a sea captain with a tattoo on his hand to a modern cowboy exploitive of the burgeoning Western mystique. Marlboro ads appearing on television series like *Rawhide* and *Tombstone Territory*—as well as national news, sports, and other network and local shows—were used to refashion for masculine esthetics a brand traditionally considered a "fancy smoke for dudes and women."[1] Moreover, long after cigarette advertising was legally banned from broadcasting and the Western was relegated to syndicated reruns, that cowboy motif continues to persuade smokers to keep Marlboro the top-selling brand of cigarettes in the United States.

What sponsors recognized in the adult Western was its ability to attract sizable audiences of potential customers; but what brought grown-ups regularly to these series was more complex. First, these alluring champions were unprecedented for television. As characters they were not only tough, but they were mature and recognizably human in their activities. It became commonplace to encounter series stars in a saloon drinking hard liquor, chatting with bargirls, or playing poker with local gamblers. These central characters broke old stereotypes. Some heroes developed romantic interests. Some sold their talents as gunfighters. Still others unashamedly lived on rewards collected for capturing outlaws dead or alive. Adult Westerns offered strong men who sweated in the summer heat and complained about the winter freeze. Occasionally, they exploded in anger. When they made mistakes, they were compelled to suffer the consequences.

In a medium that thrives on the glamorous, the adult Western offered scores of attractive young men in starring roles. Little-known but handsome actors such as James Garner, Jack Kelly, James Arness, Hugh O'Brian, Michael Ansara, Robert Culp, Steve McQueen, and Clint Walker quickly became national celebrities. Leading men well-known from motion pictures—Rory Calhoun, John Payne, Dick Powell, Ward Bond—also came to the TV Western and found renewed popularity.

The television Western was also an art form that lured and trained talented personnel behind the scenes. Many directors prominent in motion pictures now plied their trade in the video Western. Similarly, many young directors gained important experience in the TV genre before going on to achievement in feature films. Among those seasoned directors who contributed were Lewis Milestone (*Have Gun Will Travel*), R. G. Springsteen (*Trackdown, Gunsmoke, Bonanza, Laredo, Rawhide, Wagon Train*), Charles Marquis Warren (*Gunsmoke, Cimarron Strip*), Sam Fuller (*The Iron Horse, The Virginian*), Budd Boetticher (*Maverick*), and Tay Garnett (*Death Valley Days, The Legend of Jesse James, Frontier Circus, Gunsmoke, The Tall Man, Rawhide, Laramie, The Deputy, The Loner*).

Those emerging from TV Westerns to success in motion pictures included Robert Altman (*Lawman, Bronco, Sugarfoot, Maverick, Bonanza*), Andrew McLaglen (*Have Gun Will Travel, Gunslinger, Gunsmoke, The Virginian*), Boris Sagal (*Cimarron Strip, Dundee and the Culhane, A Man Called Shenandoah*), Buzz Kulik (*Have Gun Will Travel*), Sam Peckinpah (*Gunsmoke, The Rifleman, The Westerner*), and Sydney Pollack (*Frontier Circus*).[2]

After a decade dominated by situation comedies, live dramas, quiz shows, and musical-variety programs, television programmers turned in the late 1950s to filmed adventure series. Such productions allowed for a broader range of dramatic action as cameras escaped the confines of the live stage. Further, as was evident from the success of many child-oriented TV series—especially Westerns—filmed programs could be rerun and later syndicated, thereby making profits for years or decades after their premier runs.

Importantly, too, this move to film was possible because by the mid-1950s the major motion picture studios had abandoned their initial hostility to television, deciding now that there was a lucrative future in TV. The new series came from film companies long famous for quality Westerns. Among those studios and their TV series were Warner Brothers (*Maverick, Colt .45, Bronco, Cheyenne, Temple Houston, Sugarfoot*), 20th Century-Fox (*Broken Arrow, The Legend of Jesse James, Lancer, Man Without a Gun, The Loner, Daniel Boone, Custer*), United Artists (*Bat Masterson, Stoney Burke, MacKenzie's Raiders*), Metro-Goldwyn-Mayer (*Northwest Passage, A Man Called Shenandoah, The Rounders, Hondo, How the West Was Won*), Columbia (*Empire, Redigo, Jefferson Drum, The Man from Blackhawk, Two Faces West, The Outcasts, The Iron Horse*), Paramount (*Bonanza*), and Universal/MCA (*Cimmaron City, The Virginian, Destry, Tales of Wells Fargo, The Road West, Laredo, Wagon Train, Laramie, Alias Smith and Jones*). Significantly, in the case of Four Star Entertainment (*Trackdown, Law of the Plainsman, The Rifleman, Black Saddle, Johnny Ringo, The Westerner, The Big Valley, Wanted: Dead or Alive, Dick Powell's Zane Grey Theater*), the production of TV Westerns actually developed a small company not in the business of feature films—although its founders were screen stars Dick Powell, Gig Young, David Niven, and Charles Boyer—into a major force in television programming.

In this context the adult-oriented Western was a propitious genre in which to blend dramatic conflict, human insight, outdoor beauty, and subtle moralizing. But action did not disappear in the adult format. There continued to be brawls, shootouts, and quick-draw challenges to frontier manhood. The emphasis now, however, was upon fuller characterization and maturity of story line.

There were those, however, who felt such developments detrimental to the genre. From totally different perspectives actor Johnny Mack Brown and critic John Lardner lamented the emergence of the new Westerns. According to Brown, the dashing star of many B cowboy features and serials in the 1930s and 1940s,

> the films we made had a good plot and a lot of action. We had people tumbling over cliffs and swimming rivers. TV does the whole thing in a room, and they film it in two days. They just let their characters talk. We really showed them, riding to the pass . . . In TV all you've got is talk. You got New York actors in Western hats who don't know what a cow is standing around talking. . . . Where's the flying, riding, falling— the thrills of the Old West?[3]

For John Lardner the adult Western signified the ruination of a classic genre. As early as 1958 in *The New Yorker* magazine he decried "the hybrid Western" where "Freudian overtones and complexes as thick as mesquite" had supplanted the appealing simplicity of the cowboy story. A year later he was certain that the "writers of adult Westerns have become too adult for their own good, and their world, like the Roman Empire, is crumbling around them." Drawing another parallel from history Lardner warned that "the signs of Byzantine decay are unmistakable."[4]

Despite such misgivings, the adult Western did not signify the erosion of heroism or the denigration of heroic style. In fact, in the opinion of Clint Walker, the star of *Cheyenne*, the ultimate meaning of the new format was that it supplied champions for mature viewers. Writing in a fan magazine in 1955, Walker explained at length this function of the new video dramatizations.

> We are a nation of hero-worshippers and the cowboy can be anybody's hero. Now being a nation of hero-worshippers isn't bad, it's good. This is a big country and a hundred years ago when our people were pushing across the plains and over the Great Divide, every citizen had to have some of the good stuff cowboys are made of—if he wanted to survive. . . . [T]ake the real heroes we remember—men like Jim Bowie and Sam Houston and John Fremont and Wyatt Earp—they all had something of the cowboy in them. It's the kind of heroism that makes it possible for a man to live alone and at peace with himself, or to do what seems right whether it comes easy or comes hard, to stand up for what he believes in, even if it's going to be the last time he stands up. Well, from the time we Americans are little shavers sitting on grandfather's knee until the time when we're grandfathers ourselves, there's always the special need to have somebody kind of important to look up to. The problem is finding a hero everybody can agree on. Not always in the field of politics or science or education can such a man be found. Yet there seems to be one good place where such men are still bred . . . the storied West. And part and parcel of the invincibility of the West is the figure of the cowboy who inhabits it . . . as long as he and the West retain their heroic proportions, he and the Western drama won't go out of style.[5]

Although they were heroes, central characters of adult Westerns did not operate in contexts as simple as those of their child-oriented predecessors. Whatever their running time, be it 30, 60, or 90 minutes, they presented social, psychological, and moralistic complexities not found in the juvenile series. The black-and-white world yielded now to a more realistic universe tinged with ambiguous grays. As critic Cleveland Amory phrased it, "Nowadays on TV Westerns there are not only good guys and bad guys, but also in-between guys."[6]

That this was a fresh interpretation of cowboy heroics was evident in the way many actors understood their roles. Hugh O'Brian of *The Life and Legend of Wyatt Earp* explained Earp as a "lusty character, too lusty for TV. He had to have faults to be human. And I try to play him that way—relaxed until he loses his temper, then all steel springs; capable of occasional errors in judgment, but humble about them."[7]

Steve McQueen defined his role as Josh Randall in *Wanted: Dead or Alive*, noting "There's a certain honesty and realism in this series. . . . The hero isn't always a nice guy—you didn't stay alive in the Old West being nice."[8] And John Russell of *Lawman* described his character, Marshal Dan Troop, as "philosophically . . . Man doing his job, at the expense of everything else. He doesn't make himself winning or witty, or do anything else to make people like him. Unbending isn't his duty."[9]

Gene Barry of *Bat Masterson* was candid, too, in sketching the real Masterson as a Western lawman and a foppish dandy. "Bat didn't take himself too seriously. There was a little of the gimlet-eyed killer about him," noted Barry. "He proposed to relax between jobs. . . . Bat was a familiar figure in all the bars and gambling joints—and numerous romances indicate he was not one to shun the ladies." Although the video Masterson never approached the fullness of the historic figure, the series producers promised that *Bat Masterson* "will be as authentic as we can make it. . . . From the start Bat was an easygoing enforcer of law and order, refusing to take a man in unless he was definitely out of hand and a menace to himself and others."[10]

The adult Western began with the premier in September 1955 of four network series: *Gunsmoke* on CBS, *Frontier* on NBC, and *Cheyenne* and *The Life and Legend of Wyatt Earp* on ABC. Exemplifying the uncertainty with which these dramas were introduced, during its first season *Cheyenne* appeared only as part of a trilogy—the others being a program about international intrigue, *Casablanca*, and a medical series, *King's Row*—which rotated under the general title, *Warner Brothers Presents*.

Of these series premiering in 1955 only *Frontier* failed to achieve lasting popular acceptance. Ironically, as engaging programming, it was the most distinguished program of the four. Its executive producer was Worthington Miner, the TV pioneer who created and/or produced such shows as *The Goldbergs, The Toast of the Town*, and *Studio One. Frontier* was created and written by Mort Fine and David Friedkin, a writing team later responsible for the espionage series, *I Spy*, but already celebrated in radio for two gritty detective programs, *Broadway Is My Beat* and *The Lineup*, and for *Bold Venture*, an action-adventure series that starred Humphrey Bogart and Lauren Bacall. *Frontier* also featured the work of producer Matthew Rapf and emerging young directors like Sidney Lumet and Don Siegel.

However, *Frontier* was telecast on Sunday evenings opposite *The Jack Benny Program* (ranked fifth that season) and Ann Sothern's situation comedy, *Private Secretary* (ranked eleventh). Moreover, in a genre known for its appeal to rugged masculine values, Miner intended his series for a female audience. He explained in *TV Guide* that "Fifty percent of *Frontier*'s scripts are about women . . . . *Frontier* is about women with guts, not men with guns."[11] Privately, however, Miner anticipated that "since there are horses and cowhands—though without any shooting—it should reach a family audience."[12]

Although Walt Disney and his *Davy Crockett* must be given partial credit for preparing the way for the adult TV Western, the roots of the phenomenon lie elsewhere in American popular culture. Mature cowboy stories could be found in the literary work of writers like Max Brand and Clarence E. Mulford in the 1920s. William S. Hart made adult-oriented Western films in the teens and 1920s. After a hiatus during the heyday of the B Western, *Stagecoach* (1939) and *The Westerner* (1940) revived sophisticated cowboy drama—a trend accelerated in the postwar years by motion pictures such as *Duel in the Sun* (1948), *The Gunfighter* (1950), *High Noon* (1952), *Shane* (1953), and *Giant* (1955).

Television, itself, was not totally inhospitable to adult Westerns before the fall of 1955. Such programs were more uncommon on live TV than on film, perhaps because the Wild West was difficult to capture on a single stage; but it was possible to produce live Westerns. An important example was "The Death of Billy the Kid," a presentation of *The Philco Television Playhouse* on July 24, 1955, starring Paul Newman and directed by Robert Mulligan. Three years later Newman, working now with director Arthur Penn, recreated this drama as the feature film *The Left-Handed Gun*.

Adult-oriented Westerns did appear early in filmed dramatic series. During its third season on CBS, 1953-54, *The Schlitz Playhouse of Stars* regularly aired stories set in the Old West. Even earlier the syndicated anthology program *Death Valley Days*—a radio staple for almost two decades before coming to television in 1952—had adult possibilities although it tended toward quaint vignettes of pioneer days rather than mature characterizations or realistic predicaments.

The first adult Western series, predating *Gunsmoke* and even Walt Disney's programs, was the off-network series *Stories of the Century*. Syndicated in 1954, it concerned two investigators for the Southwestern Railroad—portrayed by Jim Davis and Mary Castle and later Kristine Miller—and their fictionalized encounters with infamous personalities from Western lore. Within a semidocumentary format enhanced with film footage from Republic Pictures, *Stories of the*

Century placed its central characters in the lives of desperadoes like Frank and Jesse James, Belle Starr, the "Black Jack" Ketchum gang, William Clarke Quantrill, Doc Holliday, and the Younger brothers.

The emphasis here was not a glorification of desperadoes, but a depiction of Western criminality within a biographical framework. The episode concerning Chief Crazy Horse, for example, was frank in demonstrating the culpability of the U.S. Army in the capture and death of the Sioux chieftain. It painted an ennobling image of Crazy Horse as the head of a nation—as a family man with a wife and infant son—and as a dignified leader who retained such personal pride that he chose to be shot escaping rather than face the white man's military prison.

The relative sophistication of *Stories of the Century* was not overlooked by the television industry. The series received an Emmy from the Academy of Television Arts and Sciences as the best Western or adventure series of 1954. The fact that it won the award by defeating three juvenile series—*The Roy Rogers Show, The Adventures of Wild Bill Hickok,* and *Annie Oakley*, as well as the less sophisticated *Death Valley Days*—suggests that within the TV industry there was an appreciation of the importance of Western dramatic entertainment for adult tastes.

As influential as these precursors may have been in spawning network adult Westerns, there were indications that commercial broadcasting had been moving toward this genre several years before the fall of 1955. This was especially noticeable in network radio in the early 1950s. Here in TV's sister industry CBS and NBC expended considerable effort in producing frontier dramatics intended for an older audience.

This was ironic, for only radio of all the commercial mass media consistently stultified the development of the Western. On network radio in the 1930s and 1940s the genre was treated as children's entertainment. Indeed, the cowboy champions who populated the audio Golden Age—Red Ryder, Straight Arrow, Tom Mix, The Cisco Kid, The Lone Ranger, Gene Autry, Roy Rogers, and the like—were B Western characterizations meant to attract younger listeners.[13]

This tradition was broken when *Gunsmoke* came to CBS radio in April 1952. With William Conrad as Marshal Matt Dillon, it remained a weekly production until June 1961. Flourishing in a decade when radio drama became practically nonexistent, it totalled 419 different scripts, many of which were later adapted for TV. Significantly, CBS continued into the late 1950s to experiment with adult Westerns, offering Raymond Burr as the star of *Fort Laramie* (1956), Sam Buffington in *Luke Slaughter of Tombstone* (1958), and John Dehner as the hero of both *Frontier Gentleman* (1958) and a radio version of *Have Gun—Will Travel* (1958-60).

The popularity of *Gunsmoke* on CBS appears to have spurred rival NBC radio to develop mature Westerns of its own. In the 1953-54 season James Stewart appeared as Bret Poncett, the central character of *The Six-Shooter*. The following season the network introduced a frontier physician as a pioneer hero in *Dr. Six-Gun*. These characters faced problems involving such issues as gun control, religious bigotry, and mob violence. Characters were more deeply sketched and the resolution of conflict was more ambiguous as, clearly, these programs sought to appeal to men and women. Coming as they did so late in the history of network radio, such shows were not ratings successes. Nonetheless, this experimentation familiarized NBC and CBS with the potential of the format several years before it flourished on television.

On TV the adult Western had great appeal. During its first decade it dominated popular preferences. At its height more than 60 million viewers nightly were entertained by its stories. According to one trade journal, there was so much confidence in the genre, one network reportedly held to the motto, "You can be sure if it's a Western."[14]

The mass acceptance of the Western came rapidly. During 1955 the average Nielsen rating for seven Westerns aired in prime time was 22.7, with a 37 audience share. This made the genre the fifth most popular format on television. As Table 4 illustrates, a year later the prime-time Western averaged a 26.0 rating with a 41 share, making it the leading program type in both categories.

The remarkable acceptance of the Western was no momentary fad. *Variety* reported that by October 1957 the average rating for 15 evening Westerns was 25.4—a clear 23 percent higher rating for cowboy dramas than for the other prime-time shows, which together averaged 20.7.[15]

What began as four series in late 1955 became 28 by the fall of 1959. That year, too, the networks aired as many as 17.5 hours of adult Westerns weekly. This figure represented almost one-quarter of all evening programming; and these were well-received series. One observer reported that in terms of film footage, TV Westerns by 1959 represented the equivalent of 400 feature films per year—more product than was produced during the so-called Golden Age of the B Western.[16]

Table 4   Popularity of Prime-Time Genres, 1955-56

1955 Ratings		1955 Share	
1. 60-min. variety	30.7	1. 60-min variety	40
2. Situation comedy	25.2	1. Adventure	40
3. 60-min. music	23.7	3. Situation comedy	39
3. Adventure	23.7	4. WESTERN	37
5. WESTERN	22.7	5. 60-min. music	35
6. Quiz/aud. part.	22.1	5. Suspense drama	35
7. General drama/30	21.1	5. General drama/30	35
8. Suspense drama	20.9	5. Quiz/aud. part.	35
9. General drama/60	20.8	9. General drama/60	33
10. 30-min. variety	19.6	10. 30-min. variety	30
11. 30-min. music	14.5	11. 30-min. music	23
12. Information	13.9	12. Information	25
1956 Ratings		**1956 Share**	
1. WESTERN	30.7	1. WESTERN	41
2. Situation comedy	29.5	2. Situation comedy	38
3. Suspense drama	24.8	2. Suspense drama	38
4. Adventure	21.5	4. Quiz/aud. part.	36
5. General drama/30	22.7	5. General drama/30	35
5. 60-min. music	22.7	5. 60-min. variety	35
7. 30-min. variety	22.4	7. 30-min. variety	34
8. Quiz/aud. part.	21.7	8. 60-min. music	33
9. Adventure	21.5	8. Adventure	33
10. General drama/60	22.2	8. General drama/60	33
11. Information	14.3	11. Information	25
12. 30-min. music	12.8	12. 30-min. music	22

Source: *Television Magazine*, June 1957, p. 65.

That Westerns were plentiful is obvious from a perusal of TV pro-gramming by the late 1950s. If October 3-9, 1959, was a typical week on American television, viewers in Minneapolis-St. Paul—served by six commercial stations with no overnight programming—had 81 Western programs available for viewing. Including adult and juvenile series, syndicated shows, and feature films, the daily presentations are enumerated in Table 5.

If television was flooded with Westerns, such programming was also well received. As Table 6 indicates, adult Westerns in the period 1956-65 were rated regularly among the top ten programs on television.

Table 5   Westerns on TV, Week of October 3-9, 1959

Saturday	4 movies	*Tuesday*	1 movie	
	21 series		10 series	
Sunday	2 movies	*Wednesday*	1 movie	
	12 series		5 series	
Monday	1 movie	*Thursday*	1 movie	
	7 series		3 series	
		Friday	1 movie	
			12 series	

Source: *TV Guide* (Minneapolis-St. Paul edition), October 3, 1959.

Table 6   Incidence of Westerns among Top-Rated Programs

Season Ending	Westerns in Top Ten	Rankings
1956	0	0
1957	1	No. 8
1958	5	Nos. 1, 3, 4, 6, 8
1959	7	Nos. 1, 2, 3, 4, 6, 7, 10
1960	4	Nos. 1, 2, 3, 9
1961	4	Nos. 1, 2, 3, 6
1962	3	Nos. 1, 2, 3
1963	2	Nos. 4, 10
1964	1	No. 2
1965	1	No. 1

Source: Tim Brooks and Earle March, *The Complete Directory to Prime Time Network TV Shows 1946-Present* (New York: Ballantine Books, 1985), pp. 1032-35.

In their popular years, several juvenile Westerns appeared in prime time. In the fall of 1955, for example, seven such youth-oriented series were telecast in the early evening. Within four years, however, they were totally eclipsed by mature cowboy adventures. Never again would such youth programming appear during these advantageous hours. A perusal of fall network schedules, as tabulated in Table 7, confirms that the adult variety effectively killed production of those Westerns more closely associated with B film traditions.

In terms of longevity, moreover, Table 8 indicates that the public accepted adult Westerns longer and more fully than their juvenile predecessors. Of the ten longest-running Western series in television history, only *The Lone Ranger* was intended for television.

Table 7 Network Westerns, Fall 1950-Fall 1970

Year	Adult Series/Total Hours (/)	Juvenile Series/Total Hours (/)
1950		3/(2)
1951		3/(2)
1952		2/(1)
1953		4/(2)
1954		4/(2)
1955	4/(2.5)	7/(3.5)
1956	6/(3.5)	4/(2)
1957	16/(9)	3/(1.5)
1958	24/(13.5)	2/(1)
1959	28/(17.5)	
1960	22/15.5)	
1961	13/(11)	
1962	13/(12)	
1963	9/(9.5)	
1964	6/(6.5)	
1965	13/(11)	
1966	14/(12.5)	
1967	13/(13.5)	
1968	10/(10)	
1969	6/(6.5)	
1970	4/(4.5)	

Source: Compiled by author.

In comprehending the extent to which adult Westerns dominated TV viewing, it must be remembered that the figures cited cover only the most popular network series. At their height, however, even local nonnetwork stations could choose between dozens of Western series. After several years of first runs, the more salable series were offered for off-network syndication, often under new titles. Thus, reruns of *Gunsmoke* were syndicated as *Marshal Dillon; Tales of Wells Fargo* was marketed as *Wells Fargo*; and episodes of *Wagon Train* were now called *Major Adams—Trailmaster*.

As well as reruns, stations were also able to lease Westerns that had not appeared on network TV. These offerings, syndicated directly to local markets, included *The Sheriff of Cochise*, later called *U.S. Marshal* (156 episodes), *Shotgun Slade* (78 episodes), *Two Faces West* (39 episodes), *Boots and Saddles—The Story of the Fifth Cavalry* (39 episodes), *Pony Express* (39 episodes), *MacKenzie's Raiders* (39 episodes), *Union Pacific* (39 episodes), and *Stories of the Century* (37 episodes). Furthermore, the syndicated *Death Valley Days—*

Table 8 Ten Longest-Running Westerns in TV History

Title	Length of First Run	Number of Episodes	First-Run Network Hours
Gunsmoke	Sept. 1955-Sept. 1975	640	532
Bonanza	Sept. 1959-Jan. 1973	430	431
Wagon Train	Sept. 1957-Sept. 1965	284	300
The Virginian (The Men from Shiloh)	Sept. 1962-Sept. 1971	249	373.5
Have Gun—Will Travel	Sept. 1957-Sept. 1963	226	113
The Life and Legend of Wyatt Earp	Sept. 1955-Sept. 1961	225	112.5
The Lone Ranger	Sept. 1949-Sept. 1957	221	110.5
Rawhide	Jan. 1959-Jan. 1966	217	217
Tales of Wells Fargo	Mar. 1957-Sept. 1962	198	115
The Rifleman	Sept. 1958-July 1963	168	84

Source: Larry James Gianakos, ed., *Television Drama Series Programming: A Comprehensive Chronicle, 1947-1982*, 4 vols. (Metuchen, N.J.: Scarecrow Press, 1978-83).

which between 1952 and 1975 totalled 558 half-hour shows—also was packaged for reruns under such titles as *Call of the West, Trails West, The Pioneers, Western Star Theater,* and *Frontier Adventures.*

As might be imagined, with so much cowboy theatricality on weekly TV, writers became hard-pressed to develop innovative and attractive central characters. The result was a multitude of heroic guises. There was, of course, the hero as peace officer, be he sheriff (*The Tall Man*), marshal (*Cimarron Strip*), deputy (*The Deputy*), city policeman (*Whispering Smith*), Texas Ranger (*Trackdown*), Indian agent (*Broken Arrow*), or military officer (*Custer*). One series (*The Travels of Jaimie McPheeters*) borrowed somewhat from the juvenile format, offering the West as viewed through the eyes of a 12 year old on a wagon train moving toward California.

Writers also devised champions who played the role of mercenary (*Have Gun—Will Travel*), bounty hunter (*Wanted: Dead or Alive*), rakish gambler (*Maverick*), rootless gunfighter (*Shane*), insurance investigator (*The Man from Blackhawk*), stagecoach superintendent (*The Overland Trail*), newspaperman (*Jefferson Drum*), rancher (*The Virginian*), cavalry scout (*Hondo*), railroad builder (*Union Pacific*), railroad owner (*The Iron Horse*), circus owner (*Frontier Circus*), rodeo performer (*Stoney Burke*), hotel detective (*Hotel de Paree*), civilian undercover agent for the army (*Gunslinger*), mayor (*Cimarron City*), tenderfoot law-student (*Sugarfoot*), lawyer (*Temple Houston*), and lawyers (*Dundee and the Culhane*).

Further, there was a former slave turned bounty hunter (*The Outcasts*), and a Harvard-educated Indian, now a U.S. marshal (*Law of the Plainsman*). Perhaps the most incredible central character, however, was a one-armed fast-gun-for-hire (*Tate*).

These adult Westerns ranged chronologically from the late eighteenth century (*Daniel Boone*) to the contemporary era (*Empire*). Most were rooted in towns, but some were set on sprawling ranches (*The High Chaparral*) while others moved across the Great Plains (*Wagon Train*), up the great cattle trails (*Rawhide*), or along stagecoach routes (*Stagecoach West*). Johnny Yuma was a former Confederate soldier in *The Rebel*, and William Colton was a former Union cavalry officer in *The Loner*—but both roamed the West settling other people's problems. Some meandered alone (*Wrangler*) while others rode with pals (*The Rough Riders*).

Several series focused on men with personal searches to undertake. One was looking for his criminal son (*The Guns of Will Sonnett*); another had amnesia and sought his true identity (*A Man Called Shenandoah*). The rugged hero of *Branded* was mustered unjustly out of the U.S. Army, and he now searched solemnly for vindication. The central character of *Destry*, more comedic than most Western heroes, displayed a realistic touch of caution, even cowardice, as he roamed the West looking for the men who had framed him for embezzlement.

Offering two to three dozen shows per season could be creatively exhausting for a popular series. Producers and writers learned early the imitative "recombitant style" that sociologist Todd Gitlin described as one which "collects the old in new packages and hopes for a magical synthesis."[17] Some writers simply revamped plots drawn from other genres (even from other Westerns), set them on the frontier, and converted them into Westerns. In this way in "Twenty-Four Hours to Live"—an episode of *The Texan* aired June 27, 1960—cowboy Bill Longley used classic detective techniques to deduce the identity of the killer from a gallery of likely suspects. "Brothers of the Knife," an installment of *Wichita Town* telecast October 28, 1959, took a theme familiar to gangster films—organized crime extracting protection money from innocent citizens—and told of two Mafiosi attempting to extort monthly fees from Italian immigrants living in nineteenth-century Wichita. More a modern horror story than a Western, "The Killer," a *Black Saddle* program broadcast on January 1, 1960, concerned a psychotic murderer terrorizing frontier Latigo, New Mexico.

In their search for novel programs, writers created entire series by melding other genres into the Old West. This was accomplished notably in *The Wild, Wild West*, which was both a Western set in the last century and a spy fantasy reminiscent of contemporary James Bond films. It was accomplished with less distinction in Western situation comedies such as *F Troop, Rango,* and *Pistols 'n' Petticoats.*

Still another avenue to recombitant "creativity" was to cull plots from the great literature of the past. *Bonanza* made use of themes in John Steinbeck's *Of Mice and Men* and Mary W. Shelley's *Frankenstein.* Guy de Maupassant's "Boule de Suif" became an episode of *Have Gun Will Travel.*[18] Producer Roy Huggins admitted to committing "affectionate larceny" in finding story lines for *Maverick* in Oliver Goldsmith's *She Stoops to Conquer,* Richard Brinsley Sheridan's *The Rivals,* and William Shakespeare's *Othello.*[19]

More than an outlet for reworked classic literature, however, one executive argued that the adult TV Western was itself the stuff of sublime human drama. Speaking in 1957, Richard Dorso, head of programs for Ziv Television Productions and producer of *Tombstone Territory,* contended that Westerns were

> the closest modern reflection of classical Greek tragedy, in which you did not control your fate; it was inevitable—death stood wating for you. You have the same sort of inevitability when two men face each other on the street of a frontier town and are forced to shoot it out. It's Oedidus meeting his father; it's inevitable, it must happen.[20]

Despite such strengths, even in its adult style the video Western possessed a formulaic nature. The forces of law and order invariably were victorious; continuing characters did not die; and stories carried a positive social message. Such qualities placed definite restrictions on literary imagination.

Frank Gruber, a long-time writer of Westerns and coproducer of *Tales of Wells Fargo* recognized the formula within the genre. After 15 years of creating cowboy dramas, he was convinced that there were basically seven types of Westerns: (1) the Union Pacific story—tales of the construction of railroad, telegraph, or stagecoach lines, or stories of wagon trains crossing the mountains and/or plains; (2) the Ranch story—tales of cattlemen, rustlers, and the rivalries between homesteaders and ranchers, or sheep ranchers and cattle ranchers; (3) the Empire story—focusing more closely on the large ranches or powerful families in the West, it is the Ranch story on a larger scale; (4) the Revenge story—the account of righting a wrong, even if it takes years of pursuit; (5) Custer's Last Stand—the story of the conflict between Indians and the Cavalry; (6) the Outlaw story—one that focuses, usually sympathetically, on the plight of the bandit struggling against society; (7) the Marshal story—the tale of the dedicated lawman.[21]

The degree to which Western story lines followed a predictable course was strikingly exhibited in October 1960, when CBS telecast a cowboy drama composed by a computer. After being fed details for a short sketch, the TX-O computer at the Massachusetts Institute of Technology churned out 50 plots illustrating variations possible with the given information. On the special science series, *Tomorrow*, actor David Wayne starred in samples of the computer's literary skills.[22]

THE WESTERN CHARACTER

Regardless of generic limitations on plot development, the strength of the adult Western was its characterizations of men and women in historical context. More significant than the predictability of a con- clusion was the emotional conflict the genre now presented. Unlike the melodramatic stylizations of cowboy programs meant for juvenile audiences, adult Westerns were character dramas. More than simple storytelling, they sought to draw viewers into their characters and in the process probe inner qualities and personal and moral quandaries. Here the accent was upon personality under stress and the human condition examined in the mythic past.

For NBC producer Ted Rogers, the hallmark of the adult Western was this embellishment of dramatic characters and their interrelation- ships. In 1958 he praised the newer form for the manner in which its creators took time to define individuals and show them in social ac- tion. Rogers contended that in adult Westerns "the viewer cares suf- ficiently what happens to the dramatis personae."[23]

In creating central characters whose appeal lay as much in their sympathetic qualities as their quixotic dedication, adult TV Westerns avoided the simplified imagery of the B movie tradition. Speaking of his role in bringing *Gunsmoke* from radio to television, CBS vice- president Hubbell Robinson noted in 1959:

> We worked on the character of Matt Dillon. We made him a man with doubts, confused about the job he had to do. He wondered whether he really had to do that job. We did the same for Chester and Doc. They're not just stooges for Matt.[24]

The care he showed in developing Matt Dillon was not limited to one series. Hubbell Robinson carried this same philosophy into *Have Gun—Will Travel*. Here, according to the CBS executive, the goal was to create in its central character, Paladin, a similarly complex person.

Paladin is a gun for hire, but at the same time he is a man of culture, a man with a taste for elegance. On the moral side he runs into the same confusions as [Matt] Dillon. He's not always sure of himself. He's not all black and white.[25]

Such humanization was also in the mind of Roy Huggins when he created the *Maverick* series for Warner Brothers and ABC. Huggins intentionally developed leading men who broke all the rules of the traditional Western hero. The Maverick brothers and their kin were recognizable types. When enduring insults from a bully of obvious superior strength, the Mavericks worried less about male pride and more about pain; if faced with a robber's six-gun after a profitable game of poker, the Mavericks readily surrendered their winnings. The brothers followed the advice of their "Pappy" that "work is all right for killin' time, but its a shaky way to make a livin'."

With a relaxed fatalism absent from most series leads, the Mavericks were iconoclastic. Speaking in 1958, Huggins outlined the Maverick persona as "he's a little bit of a coward, he's not solemn, he's greedy and not above cheating a little, he's indifferent to the problems of others. He's something of a 'gentle grafter,' but we couldn't use the title because O. Henry used it first."[26]

In such a manner principals in the adult Western may have remained heroic to viewers, but their achievements were tempered, even enhanced, by the human vulnerability they possessed. More than granite symbols of right against wrong, they operated as thinking, feeling grownups with sensibilities that were integral to their social functions.

On *The Rifleman* the personality of Lucas McCain outweighed his expertise in firearms. Although his rifle was a violent, if discriminate, tool of pioneer life, the quality that made the series last six seasons was the fatherly, protective love that McCain, as a widower, demonstrated for his young son; and the concern that McCain, as a citizen with roots planted in a frontier community, exhibited toward his town and those living in and around it.

In Josh Randall of *Wanted: Dead or Alive*, audiences accepted for three years a traditionally despised Western type: the bounty hunter; but Randall challenged the stereotype of the bounty hunter as grizzled, mean, and antisocial. He was likeable, caring, and even self-sacrificing at times. True to the American business ethic, Randall was an ambitious young professional whose enterprise was capturing wanted criminals. Tough and defensive he could be, but Randall was a self-starter, a hard worker seeking to get ahead; and ultimately he worked in the name of law and order.

If McCain was protective and Randall was ambitious, Vint Bonner of *The Restless Gun* was fashioned along more familiar lines. Bonner was created as a "sympathetic working cowhand, an itinerate who spends six months in one town, a year in another, and who is pretty well known as a dependable, nice guy." John Payne, who played Bonner for two years on NBC, suggested that his character was an ingratiating one. "People sort of naturally gravitate towards Bonner when they've got problems," he told *TV Guide* in 1958, "and Bonner tries to solve them as best he can. If there is such a thing as a next-door neighbor in a Western, that's Vint Bonner."[27]

Some of the more challenging characterizations occurred in those few programs that focused upon outlaws as central characters. The noted film director Don Siegel was closely involved in a series based on the life of Jesse James. *The Legend of Jesse James* lasted only the 1965-66 season, failing in great part because its writers were unable to make the notorious robber and killer into a believably sensitive character whose basic concerns were for the common man. Reviewing the effort, Cleveland Amory in *TV Guide* chided its producers for trying "to make, out of a robbing hood, Robin Hood." He continued, "The trouble is that the producers, having decided to give us an outlaw for a hero, then proceeded in script after script to make him, if not an in-law, at least not all bad."[28]

More successful at placing a bad man at the center of a series was *The Tall Man*. On NBC from 1960 to 1962, this undertaking treated fictionally the relationship between Sheriff Pat Garrett and Billy the Kid. Again it was necessary to adjust the historical image of a notorious murderer, William H. Bonney, to make him a personality with whom, it was hoped, viewers would identify. Clu Gulager, who portrayed Billy the Kid, claimed the program depicted the interaction between a fatherly Garrett, "a man of vision, but a human being . . . with all the foibles of a human being," and the Kid whom "some day he will be forced to kill." In sketching Billy the Kid, Gulager touched upon the sympathetic nature that all adult Westerns sought to instill in their central characters:

> Pat Garrett loved Billy. . . . The Mexican people loved him. He was lovable—except that, at certain times, he became mean and vicious. He killed twenty-one men. Some of these slayings were justified, some were

not. . . . We're not whitewashing Billy. But at the same time, we are not showing him as nothing but a vicious killer. He had a gentle side.[29]

In terms of sustained interest in Western characterizations, the most successful production was *Gunsmoke*. Each weekly episode focused on a complex situation in which series regulars interacted with strangers and the townspeople of Dodge City. Kitty Russell, the tough owner of the Long Branch saloon, epitomized the tension between social respectability and the demands of a single woman making a living on the frontier. Doc Adams possessed the classic gruff exterior masking a vulnerable, self-sacrificing professionalism. For dramatic relief, as well as occasional law enforcement purposes, Chester Goode and later Festus Hagen were deputy marshals better skilled in brewing a pot of coffee or unconsciously adding a humorous tinge to Dodge City life.

The center of the moral universe in *Gunsmoke* was Matt Dillon. Slow to anger and aware of what drove men to criminality in the 1870s, the good marshal presided cautiously over his jurisdiction. In an installment of the CBS documentary series, *The 20th Century* ("The Western Hero," broadcast March 19, 1963), narrator Walter Cronkite aptly described Dillon as "more of a large, armed scoutmaster in a world of maladjusted human beings."

With regulars as well as weekly heavies, Dillon was forthright but not without well-planned shortcomings. He did not know all the answers; he sometimes misjudged people; he could get angry; he sometimes needed other people to complete his tasks. In fact, the creators of *Gunsmoke* were careful to keep the marshal an identifiable character capable of mistakes. Producer-director Norman Macdonnell in 1958 explained that "as soon as your lead becomes a hero, you're in trouble." Macdonnell admitted that when Matt Dillon starts to become unrealistically invincible it is time to "fix him," to write a script where "poor old Matt gets outdrawn and outgunned and pulls every dumb trick in the book. It makes him, and us, human."[30] That prescription for commonality lasted into the last years of the series. According to John Mantley, producer of *Gunsmoke* in the early 1970s, "Matt is fallible. And the ordinary guy can say, 'He's just like me.' "[31]

To label a Western as "adult" did not imply that its language or imagery broke network restrictions regarding "good taste." Neither did it suggest that such a program approximated the frankness found in Western motion pictures at the time. The adult Western drew from the theatrical tradition of television where throughout the 1950s live dramas were aired each evening.

Of course, some adult Westerns were more complex than others. *Gunsmoke*, for example, probed character with subtlety and sensitivity, while *The Life and Legend of Wyatt Earp* was often exaggerated and obvious in its representation of frontier predicaments. Furthermore, there were variations within individual series. For example, in *Johnny Ringo*, which lasted for 38 episodes on CBS in 1959-60, there was a wide range of imagery. On the sophisticated side, individual episodes involved Sheriff Ringo in social issues such as the coddling of criminals ("The Hunters" on October 29, 1959), racial and ethnic prejudice ("Shoot the Moon," aired June 2, 1960), and political assassination ("The Assassins," aired February 18, 1960). One story involved a lonely woman whose flirtations resulted in several violent deaths ("Four Came Quietly," aired January 28, 1960). Another episode, written by Richard Levinson and William Link, revolved about death and a coach that had disappeared years earlier ("Ghost Coach," aired November 12, 1959).

However, the series had its simpler moments. In "Killer, Choose a Card" on June 9, 1960, Ringo used a silly trick to save an old woman sentenced to hang for committing a murder. He accomplished this by having the woman fake her own suicide, then appear dressed as a ghost before four men he suspected. Shaken by this "apparition" in a white dress and covered with white facial powder, the true murderer cried out a confession.

Even more out of character was Ringo's performance in "Kid with a Gun" where he became the first (and possibly only) "singing" adult TV Western hero. As televised on Christmas eve in 1959, Ringo helped a young girl recite her "Now I lay me down to sleep" bedtime prayers, then followed with a lullaby—lushly embellished with an orchestral backing—while she lay tucked in bed. Before playing Ringo actor Don Durant, who composed the song, had been a singer with the Ray Anthony band. His performance in this episode was more worthy of Roy Rogers or Gene Autry than the serious-minded Sheriff Ringo.

To remain viable, television producers had to understand the limitations imposed upon a mass entertainment product by the mass audience. Most stations were reluctant to broadcast material they felt might offend local sensibilities. Most sponsors, too, did not want their products associated with dramatic innovations that might be disconcerting or frustrating to audiences.

For their part, viewers seemed to prefer predictability in the entertainment entering their homes via television. As is usually the case with American popular culture, the mass audience preferred the familiarity of the conventional. Viewers usually made hit shows out of series that offered formula and fashion instead of originality.

Statistics indicated, moreover, that the popularity of many adult Westerns rested with children. In the case of the long-running *Bonanza*, for example, Nielsen ratings in 1961 showed that 35 percent of its audience was comprised of viewers 17 years old and younger.[32] Thus, at a time when citizen groups and government agencies were railing against violence and sexual imagery on TV, executives from the network level downward were sensitive to public criticism.

Tempted as they might be, production companies were not able to sustain Western characters whose frankness went beyond the limits of taste to which television adhered. Illustrative of this reality was the case of *The Californians*. As reported in *TV Guide*, the series underwent major alterations in characterization and scope as a result of viewer and sponsor upset. When it premiered in the fall of 1957, *The Californians* concerned life in San Francisco's unruly Barbary Coast section. It attempted to depict rather starkly the brutality, lawlessness, and racial tension prevalent in gold rush days. It also focused flatteringly on a young newspaperman from the East and on a band of vigilantes he joined to establish law and order. As the central character, the vigilante Easterner was soon replaced by a marshal—but he was compromised by being the owner of a gambling establishment filled with drinking and gambling patrons as well as women apparently of easy virtue.

Such characterization might have succeeded in feature films, but as a TV project it met with quick disapproval. Sponsor, advertising agency, network, and series producer—all compelled the writers to tone down their representations. Dancehall girls were pushed further into the background. The vigilante element was discontinued. Shot glasses and gaming tables were deemphasized, and violence and rough language were tempered.

According to *TV Guide*, "the sponsor was dissatisfied with the Old West as it was, and wanted it altered along socially acceptable lines." Within a few months the central character's "traits began to evaporate and he became virtually indistinguishable from all other TV cowboys."[33] However, with such alterations the program was able to remain on NBC for two years.

While the adult Western had boundaries it had to respect, it was still a creditable drama. Relative to the juvenile series, moreover, it was a sizable step forward in programming maturity. Indeed, the adult Western stood out in three important directions: (1) its emphasis upon psychological considerations, often as a result of the fuller characterization that it displayed; (2) the quantity and quality of violence that it demonstrated; and (3) the generally more complex handling of the genre and its traditional themes. In analyzing these features, a more complete understanding of the video Western can be gained.

THE PSYCHOLOGICAL TONE

In contrast to the melodramatic purposefulness that marked B Western types, heroes and villains in the newer format could appear tentative, confused, or even psychotic. No longer trite shoot-'em-ups, adult TV Westerns often were psychological studies.

This was well understood by contemporaries who frequently commented on the emotional tenor of many series. The noted director and video personality, Alfred Hitchcock, quipped in 1957 that "there seem to be no more villains—now we have only good guys and neurotics."[34] The president of one TV production company praised the Western in 1958 as "emotional" drama so filled with character development that often there was "not a shot fired or a horse in sight."[35] Producer Aaron Spelling considered it a compliment when a sponsor compared his *Johnny Ringo* to one of the most celebrated dramatic series in television history, remarking, "That's no western. It's a regular *U.S. Steel*."[36]

The producers of *The Life and Legend of Wyatt Earp* immodestly linked their television series to the tradition of precedent-setting psychological Western films such as *Shane* and *High Noon*. In describing the enduring qualities of adult Western movies, they suggested that *Wyatt Earp* possessed similar greatness.

> In the past few years a few Westerns have been realized which deal with their subjects in an adult fashion. The characters portrayed are believable men and women, some good, some bad, but most displaying a mixture of strength and weakness in varying proportions. The other elements of the Western may be present—Indians, buffaloes, cowboys, etc.—but life is not portrayed as an eternal succession of these elements, one in perpetual pursuit of another. The names of these movies, significantly, are well-known and have escaped the usual fate of the typical grade-B Westerns—the fate of lost identity.[37]

The psychological flair in these programs was depicted in a multitude of ways. "Black Harvest" was an emotive episode of *Johnny Ringo* aired April 7, 1960. It concerned an older man who kept his wife in constant terror because he feared she might leave him for a younger man. "Dos Pinos," an installment of *The Westerner* on November 4, 1960, told of three sadistic drifters who shot and wounded a local rancher and were now taking bets on whether he would die before morning.

In an episode of *Wanted: Dead or Alive*, the psychological emphasis was recognizable in the remorse and soul-searching of Josh Randall after apparently killing a young man he mistook for a wanted criminal. The entire *Branded* series, treating as it did a soldier wrongly accused of cowardice and ignobly mustered out of the Army, was a psychological study of a frontier man seeking restoration of his self-respect and social acceptability.

In probing the inner constitution of its characters, the TV Western sought a more complete understanding of the human spirit. Knowing what made Paladin, the Cartwrights of *Bonanza*, or the Maverick brothers "tick" became integral to an appreciation of these series. Sometimes there was little mystery. The opening scenes of *Branded* always showed Jason McCord being stripped of his rank, having his sword broken, and ignobly leaving the fort where he once had been a captain in the U.S. Cavalry—all this while a chorus sang in the background about the court-martial that had mistakenly convicted him of cowardice in the face of battle.

In the case of the short-lived series, *The Loner*, the psychological boundaries of the program were immediately delineated when a narrator described the character of William Colton, a disillusioned former officer in the Union Army who now rode the West in search of meaning:

> In the aftermath of the blood-letting called the Civil War, thousands of ruthless, restless, searching men travelled West. Such a man is William Colton. Like the others, he carried a blanket roll, a proficient gun, and a dedication to a new chapter in American history: the opening of the West.

Usually, however, viewers discovered the inner qualities of central characters by observing their reactions to situational pressures. Most poignantly this was the pattern in "Squeeze Play," an episode of *The Rifleman* telecast December 3, 1962. Here was the cowboy champion with his personal values exposed. Lucas McCain openly discussed his private reasons for settling on his present ranch. He also spoke his fatherly love for his young son. McCain also testified to his strongly held belief that a man must live by principles. Lamenting that for too many people "sometimes it's only a word," he explained that "there has to be something we live and feel, not just something we talk about."

McCain had his convictions tested when an unscrupulous land speculator tried to force him to sell the ranch. He was brutalized by thugs. His fence was knocked down and his house was set on fire. Even his friends urged him to capitulate. In a final scene at McCain's ranch, he was savagely beaten by three burly employees of the speculator. But his fortitude in withstanding such punishment exasperated the antagonist who called off the intimidation. Still, before his adversaries left the ranch, a bruised but undaunted McCain demanded $5 owed him for replacement of the broken fence. It was an act of inner courage and integrity.

While such presentations probed the mentality of settlers on the frontier, experts on the history of the American West discounted these video series as Hollywoodized distortions of reality. After all, this was Southern California in the 1950s, not Deadwood, Tombstone, or Carson City in the nineteenth century. Whether set in the Badlands of the Dakota Territory (*The Dakotas*), the arid deserts of the Southwest (*Trackdown*), or any spot along the Oregon and Santa Fe trails (*Wagon Train*), their actual backgrounds were usually California locations such as the Conejo Ranch, Mt. Whitney at Lone Pine, Big Bear Lake, Pioneer Town in the Mojave desert, Gene Autry's La Placeritas Ranch, and Squaw Valley. Occasionally, however, series were filmed at facilities near Gallup, New Mexico, and Tucson, Arizona.[38]

Furthermore, the handsome and principled heroes of the video screen hardly resembled the denizens of the authentic Wild West. The true Johnny Ringo did not look like the handsome Don Durant; the real Ringo was tall and skinny and died of tuberculosis in his mid-thirties. Wyatt Earp never rose above the rank of assistant marshal in Dodge City, partly because of his friendship with the psychopathic criminal, Doc Holliday, and Doc's disreputable girlfriend, "Big Nose" Kate. Bat Masterson was a professional gambler, as well as a law officer, who cautioned against the quick draw—"Take your time and don't miss," was his real advice to deputies. And William Bonney, Jr. —the legendary Billy the Kid—was in reality a homicidal transplant from the slums of New York City who murdered 21 men in the New Mexico territory before he was shot down.

Veteran cowboy actor Tim McCoy, himself a former wrangler born at the end of the last century, discussed the inaccuracies of the filmic Western hero. Interviewed in Mike McElreath's documentary film in 1972, *Brave New Cowboy*, McCoy differentiated between the mythical and the actual.[39]

> There were never heroes out West ever. They've been made heroes by books that have been published about them. And then when they put them on the screen, they were more glorified heroes than they were even in the books. The fellows who were supposed to be the gunmen and the deputy marshals in most of those towns were nothing but a bunch of tin-horn gamblers. It's quite true they put a star on so they could carry a gun and protect themselves. And they all had an interest in every gambling joint and whorehouse in town.

Few series attempted to deal realistically with the historic West. When they did, however, it could cause consternation. In the fall of 1959, for example, the producers of *The Life and Legend of Wyatt Earp* aired an episode depicting the historic Johnny Ringo as a coward who refused to stand up to Marshal Earp. This portrayal, however, upset the producers of the television series *Johnny Ringo*. They set about to write an episode in which Earp and Doc Holliday backed down in a disagreement with Ringo.

With its docudrama approximation *Stories of the Century* had the sense of historical reenactment, but for authenticity nothing surpassed *The Real West* and its interpretation of frontier realities. *The Real West* was an installment of NBC's prestigious documentary series, *Project XX*. It was telecast originally on March 29, 1961, but it was rerun several times thereafter. Cited by historian A. William Bluem as "among the finest Theme Documentaries created for American television,"[40] it examined the American wilderness that was settled between 1840 and 1900.

The Real West examined the unglamorous verities of the hinterland as it was being occupied by hardy pioneers from points East. Through film footage and still pictures, narrator Gary Cooper argued that the Wild West was a literary fiction created for thrill-seeking Eastern readers by pulp writers like Ned Buntline. In fact, according to Cooper, the West "had hardly really got woolly" when Eastern civilization began to arrive.

> For one thing, too many men had burned too many beans. The winters seemed longer, and the lonesome seemed thicker. So they wrote home for Mary Ann. And when she arrived—by the thousands—respectable

and strong-willed, she said, "We've got to make this a fit country to raise kids in." And then the West knew it was going to have to start shaving on Sunday and stop wearing its galluses looped across its butt. Gold dust had gotten gritty to the taste and was mighty thin nourishment. A can of peaches looked real good to a man who had been on a steady diet of his own or his neighbor's beef.

Soon the railroad, law, town planning, schools and colleges, and religion were firmly rooted on the frontier. From the implantation of high culture to the importation of nontippable spitoons, Eastern civility quickly modified the Wild West. And it was desired, for in the words of one pioneer, it was part of "all that is needful to transform the wilderness into Arcadia."

The video Western, like its counterparts in radio, motion pictures, and literature, was designed to appeal to the present day for, as TV scholar Horace Newcomb has noted, "television has made the Western into a lens through which we can view our contemporary culture."[41] If it probed character and psychological construct, it was because viewers preferred this deeper dramatic scope to earlier cowboy forms. If its champions were virtuous and handsome and athletic, it was because this was how mid-twentieth-century Americans envisioned their nation-building progenitors. And if it fictionalized an environment in which morality always triumphed, it was because such myths explained and justified the moral tenets of modern society. Self-flattering and reinforcing, the mythic West depicted in the adult Western was at base a metaphor for the United States in the 1950s and 1960s.

VIOLENCE AND THE ADULT WESTERN

Violence was an integral component of most adult Westerns. In many cases it was promised by recurring scenes that each week introduced various series. In *Gunsmoke* it was the view of Matt Dillon striding into the street to draw against a challenger. *Wichita Town* opened with three bullets smashing through the glass window of Marshal Mike Dunbar's office. In *The Rifleman* it was Lucas McCain firing a dozen rifle shots in rapid succession, twirling his pump-action weapon in the air, then grasping it manfully in one strong hand.

Paladin of *Have Gun—Will Travel* always pointed his gun directly at the TV viewer, spouted a few intelligent sentences, then holstered it with military precision. With Christopher Colt in *Colt .45*, the violence was promised with a quick draw, a sudden turn toward the camera, and a rapid firing of shots to spell out the name of the series.

Several programs by their titles indicated violence. As well as those cited above, series like *Shotgun Slade, The Restless Gun, Yancy Derringer, Gunslinger*, and *The Guns of Will Sonnett* exploited firearms from their opening credits. Although the hero of *The Adventures of Jim Bowie* did not use a gun, he was the inventor of the Bowie knife, and he regularly displayed that menacing instrument. Only *Man Without a Gun*, a syndicated program in the late 1950s that concerned a crusading newspaper publisher in the Old West, and *Gun Shy*, a short-lived Western spoof in 1983, suggested an aversion to violence.

Ballistic savagery permeated all Westerns. It grew inevitably from the scenario of a world where adult men moved about their society with firearms strapped to their hips and rifles and shotguns holstered on their saddles. This was the visualization of a civilization on the verge of anarchy. Yet such dramatic representation was acceptable to American audiences. As one observer explained it in 1958, the violent imagery in the Western was understandable in terms of history and justifiable in terms of the debt contemporary society owed to the past.

> Cruel the Western is and violent, but rustling, fence-cutting, monopolizing the water supply, and such situations upon which script writers freely draw, were threats to human subsistence. Out of such great struggle all through history came the safety which allowed societies to flourish and to build.[42]

Ironically, in several series these deadly weapons were revered as well-crafted objects of veneration. *The Life and Legend of Wyatt Earp* featured Earp's imposing Buntline Special, a customized handgun with a 16-inch barrel. Josh Randall in *Wanted: Dead or Alive* wore a sawed-off, pump-action 44/40 carbine on his right hip. Sheriff Johnny Ringo carried a replica of the LeMat, a French firearm designed in 1863 to combine a six-shooter and a rifle. In a photographic essay entitled "Arms and the Western Men," *TV Guide* in 1960 glamorously highlighted seven of these "most prominent players—the firearms that help Western heroes repel villains and attract viewers."[43]

Significantly, the emphasis upon firearms in TV Westerns helped spur gun sales in the United States. By late 1958 weapons manufacturers were turning out 10,000 Western-type guns monthly to meet consumer demand. While admitting to the relationship between television programming and the rise in firearm sales, one manufacturer quickly added that "Western TV shows, as well as Western movies, should be judged not on the fact that guns are employed, but on whether the basic plot brings the Golden Rule out convincingly to youngsters who are watching it."[4][4]

The veneration of firearms generated via the TV Western was in part symptomatic of a society locked in political and economic fear and reliant upon military strength to enforce its will in Cold War affairs. The genre always possessed a militaristic flavor. As British scholar Herbert L. Jacobson wrote, even in the politically isolationist 1920s and 1930s—the boom period for theatrical B Westerns—through films the "cowboy tradition helped keep alive the military spirit, which twice in a generation saved the country from domination by an autocracy bred on a Teutonic warrior tradition."[4][5] But now at a time of East-West confrontation when Americans were unused to a consistent military role in global politics, the militaristic TV Western offered explanations and justification.

Among the more instructive and violent adult series was *Have Gun—Will Travel*, and this was ironic for as a Western it had a unique veneer of urbane sophistication. As portrayed by Richard Boone, Paladin often quoted poetry and made pithy references to great literature. He knew fine wine and was a connoisseur of *haute cuisine*. Dressed impeccably and conversing with elegant men and women, Paladin was thoroughly a gentleman. Most episodes commenced with him enjoying the luxurious lifestyle of the Hotel Carlton in San Francisco: dining with a beautiful lady of social standing, smoking an elegant panatella, deeply involved in a game of chess, or preparing for an evening at the theater. Yet, as with the society entertained by TV Westerns, out of this facade of civility came amazing violence—and all in the name of justice.

Paladin was a mercenary, a hired gunslinger employed by the defenseless as protection against a variety of threats. Dressed now in funerary black trousers with matching black shirt and hat, Paladin's alter ego emerged as a tough if rational avenger intent upon establishing justice. His dedication to right was so pronounced, in fact, he occasionally operated free of charge, resolving an inequity he inadvertently encountered or undertaking a purely personal vendetta.

That Paladin could hold his own in the mayhem of the Wild West was ably demonstrated in "The Misguided Father," an episode aired February 27, 1960. Here the heroic Paladin dealt with a pathological killer, the unstable son of a timber baron who shot men impulsively. During the program Paladin was knocked unconscious from his horse and later engaged in a vicious fistfight that lasted one minute of screen time. But the most striking aspect of the story was the incidence of murder. Counting both the dead bodies portrayed and the murders ascribed to the son and others, the final body count was impressive: the father killed one man; the son murdered ten; and Paladin slew the son. Despite the omnipresence of slaughter, Paladin maintained his emotional balance. In a most dispassionate tone, with his Colt .45 revolver still warm from having shot the crazed son, Paladin chided the distraught father: "My bullet, your mistakes."

The suave performance of Paladin, able to slay a man in one second and proffer wisdom in the next, marked not only *Have Gun—Will Travel*, but the adult Western in general as a stereotypical masculine genre. There were few female heroics in these TV series. The brawls, shootouts, and other forms of violence were products of male social prerogatives. David Dortort, the producer of *Bonanza*, consciously eschewed female interference in his manly Western. Speaking of the leading character in the series, the patriarchal Ben Cartwright, Dortort explained that "he is not led around by the nose by anybody. We do not have any Moms built into our show—or for that matter, any women. We are, as it were, anti-Momism."[4 6]

James Arness also understood *Gunsmoke* and its viewing audience in terms of gender. "People like Westerns because they represent a time of freedom," he remarked in 1958. "A cowboy wasn't tied down to one place or to one woman. When he got mad he hauled off and slugged someone. When he drank he got good and drunk." In the interpretation of TV's Matt Dillon, "that is why they tune in on Western shows, to escape from conformity. They don't want to see a U.S. marshal come home and help his wife wash the dishes."[4 7]

Indeed, no central character in a video Western ever came home to help his wife with housework. Housework was unmanly labor for a frontiersman. Although widower Lucas McCain occasionally was shown preparing meals, he soon taught his young son to cook, and more often than not, this rifleman came home to dinner made by his child.

More significantly, however, few Western champions actually had a wife. There were prominent widowers such as Lucas McCain in *The Rifleman*, Murdoch Lancer in *Lancer*, and Ben Cartwright of *Bonanza*; and several heroes like Marshal Jim Crown in *Cimarron Strip* and lawyer Clay Culhane in *Black Saddle* had eligible women regularly interested in them. Except for middle-aged John Cannon—the patriarchal ranch-owner of *The High Chaparral* who was a widower before marrying the young Mexican cattle heiress, Victoria Montoya—there was little evidence of domesticity in the lives of TV Western heroes, even though these men frequently risked their lives to safeguard familial institutions and values.

If they were unmarried, moreover, these Westerners relished their bachelorhood. The closest a bachelor/hero ever came to being married on a series was in "Three's a Crowd," an episode of *Laredo* aired October 14, 1965. Here Chad Cooper, part of the closely knit trio of young Texas Rangers featured on the program, actually became engaged, resigned his job, and prepared to leave town with his fiancee. However, his Ranger buddies needed him in a fight against warring Comanches, and rather than renounce the ties of male bonding, Cooper abandoned his sweetheart at the stagecoach, ended his engagement, and explained that "there are certain things a man's got to do."

As well as their scarcity as heroines in adult TV Westerns, women also were rarely the perpetrators or targets of physical violence. For the most part, men fought and killed one another. Certainly, barroom girls came in for occasional rough treatment at the hands of drunken cowboys or aggressive gamblers, but this usually meant nothing more than abusive language or a few slaps and pushes. The most abused character in this regard was Kitty Russell of *Gunsmoke* who several times each season had to contend with uncivil customers at her Long Branch saloon; but she lasted 20 seasons essentially untouched.

There were, however, striking exceptions to this pattern. Occasionally women were killed in adult Westerns. This happened to a kindly grandmother in the opening scene of "Rope of Sand," a *Laramie* episode telecast February 16, 1960—mercilessly shot down with her husband by a robber interrupted while stealing their life savings. In "Die Twice," an installment of *Johnny Ringo* on January 21, 1960, the murder of a young wife was even more brutal. Here the woman was shot in the back by her outlaw husband as she ran from him directly toward the camera. The *coup de grace* was delivered by the outlaw's sidekick who picked up the slain woman's handkerchief, smelled its perfumed aroma, and while glancing at her corpse on the ground quipped wryly, "What a waste."

In "Three for One," an installment of *Whispering Smith* telecast on July 3, 1962, brutality against a woman was both implied and visualized. Upon discovering a robbed stagecoach with its driver and male passenger dead, Smith and his assistant speculated on the fate of the attractive female passenger apparently abducted by the murderers.

> Assistant: (handling woman's parasol) Looks like there was a woman
> in that coach.
> Smith: Um hum, there was.
> Assistant: Think they took her hostage?
> Smith: They took her, all right. They headed south, right through
> those hills.
> Assistant: (pointing to dead men) Smitty, what about them?
> Smith: Nothing more can happen to them. I'm not so sure about
> that girl.

Later in the story the violence became more graphic. When cornered by the lawmen, one murderer grabbed the woman, held a knife menacingly at her neck, and warned, "OK, mister, drop that gun or she's gonna get it right in the throat."

Less murderous, but nonetheless devastating, was the antifemale imagery in "Jeff," the premier episode of *The Westerner*. This powerful series lasted only a half-season, but it was critically acclaimed at the time as it was produced and occasionally written and directed by Sam Peckinpah—the filmmaker whose Western career included early writing and directing for *Gunsmoke* and *The Rifleman* and later directing such controversially violent features as *The Wild Bunch, Ride the High Country,* and *Bring Me the Head of Alfredo Garcia.*

As aired on September 30, 1960, "Jeff" offered a theme regularly treated in Peckinpah Westerns, the search for personal dignity. Set in a grim, barely populated barroom the episode concerned a sadistic bar owner and his masochistic girlfriend, a dispirited prostitute whom he dominated. Physically and emotionally abused by the antagonist, the young woman long ago had abandoned her sense of dignity. Despite an earnest intervention—complete with a proposal of marriage—by the virtuous hero of the series, she opted to remain with her "master." "Jeff" was a humiliating picture of rejected respectability and the triumph of sin and submission.

Reviewers did not dismiss the episode or the series as run-of-the-mill. The critic for *The Hollywood Reporter* was pleased with the program, terming it "breathless theater" and "a great show, a standout series, and its strongest competition in the weeks ahead will be its own standards."[48] But in *Variety* the reviewer seemed ill at ease when he described "Jeff" as "tawdry" and "a shocker," a program filled with "peephole interest and violent displays," and carried out within a "sickening atmosphere."[49] Two decades later a critic for the Los Angeles *Times* suggested that *The Westerner* "was maybe the only honest portrait of a cowboy that ever got onto film."[50]

SOPHISTICATION OF THE GENRE

While it flourished on American television in the 1950s and 1960s, the Western was compelling fictional amusement. More than simple diversion, however, the Western as a cultural construct also operates as an educative conduit through which important social and personal lessons are disseminated. In this way the Western is parabolical. Set primarily in the past where history may be manipulated to serve contemporary purposes, the genre is filled with symbols and symbolic actions relating directly to the popular mentality of the society accepting it as entertainment.

How often has the genre portrayed the value of responsible social freedom? How often have democratic themes of tolerance, equality, and human dignity emerged as the moral of a cowboy drama? How frequently has the Western profferred those symbols of modern life—church, fence, schoolhouse, family, ranch house, jail, graveyard—as guideposts in the establishing of roots and the flourishing of organized social life? How often have such capitalistic tenets as hard work, individuality, and self-reliance appeared as emulable characteristics of the Western hero?

Certainly, in the case of the United States in the 1950s and 1960s, the genre was intended as neither calculated indoctrination nor historical reconstruction. Yet, just as surely as the mythology of ancient Greece and Rome explained and sanctified the social arrangements of those civilizations, televised tales of the Old West were meaningful secularized American myths that analagously served their particular public.

In the juvenile format, moralizing factors were heavy-handed. With Sunday school frankness, champions were good and villains were evil. The adult TV Western, however, always allowed for broader manipulation of its generic components. Younger minds might appreciate the incidental action; but the complexity of its stories and characters was intended for grown-ups to appreciate.

A favorite motif of the Western has always been redemption of the fallen, the notion that in the West a person could rediscover himself or herself, could make a new start in a new land, could escape the confusion of earlier failure in the East and find social salvation in the forgiving West. The theme has obvious roots in Christian theology and, more immediately, in the advance of U.S. democracy and political hegemony from New England to the West Coast. In "The Colter Craven Story," as it appeared on *Wagon Train* on November 23, 1960, this motif was powerfully communicated.

As directed by John Ford, the master director of Western motion pictures such as *Stagecoach, Red River, Fort Apache*, and *She Wore a Yellow Ribbon*, this story told of an Eastern doctor whose self-confidence was shattered by his experiences during the Civil War when at the battle of Shiloh most of his patients died.[51] Now an alcoholic and a broken man, Dr. Colter Craven came to the frontier to forget in alcohol and anonymity.

The theme of this episode was that through successful acceptance of responsibility the dispirited could obtain redemption. Major Seth Adams, leader of the wagon train, had no sympathy for the drunken self-pity exhibited by Craven. Himself the essential pioneer, full of purpose and discipline and out to create a new Eden, Adams refused to indulge the fallen physician. In harsh words he blasted Craven's weakness, calling him

> the eighth wonder of the world—a living man without one single solitary gut. Who do you think you are to sit in judgment of yourself? What makes you think that you ought to be infallible? You aren't the only one who was at Shiloh. You're not the only man who wanted to push his memories back into a bottle and put the cork in. What right have you got to make yourself personally responsible for the war?

The program reached its climax when the inebriated doctor was compelled to perform a Caesarian delivery, failure to operate meaning certain death for both mother and child. To overcome Craven's initial reluctance, Adams related the story of Ulysses S. Grant's personal redemption—from being dismissed from the military for alcoholism, to his recovery to become general of the Union Army and later president of the United States. "He had a lot more responsibility than you, Doc," prodded Adams, and "he used that responsibility to redeem himself. It isn't often a man gets a second chance. What are you going to do?" His hands now steadied and his self-confidence restored, Craven saved mother and child and himself through this surgery in the wild.

This was entertaining television, and it was enhanced by the reuniting of that trio responsible for so many classic Western feature films—John Ford, Ward Bond, and John Wayne in his only TV dramatic performance, an uncredited cameo role as General William T. Sherman.[52] More importantly, however, in this diverting hour millions of viewers were offered a familiar lesson. In the image of a reprobate physician rescuing himself there was an impressive model for countless "Colter Craven types" needing encouragement to overcome personal calamities. Even for those without such debilitation, the story reaffirmed the need for continued self-control and social responsibility.

The writer who best understood the symbolic potentialities of the broadcast Western was John Meston. One of the originators of *Gunsmoke*, he wrote 378 scripts for its TV and radio versions. Meston's compositions were deceptively simple, distinguishable by their subtle glorification of the civilizing process operating within the pioneer town, and by their sensitivity to human character and personality in conflict with unforgiving nature.

In Meston's world view, Dodge City was man's hope in the wilds. There may have been disruptive elements in the town, but it was still preferable to the naked brutality of the hinterland. Within Dodge City there were laws and cooperative arrangements. This was organized society, not Rousseau's state of nature. Here the social contract of John Locke and the spirit of the laws of Montesquieu blended to offer protection and, consequently, hope for future survival. A citizen had to abandon some freedoms to cohabit in Dodge City; but what a person surrendered to join civility was the anarchistic freedom of the wild animal within the kill-or-be-killed natural world, the freedom to perish at the hands of predators or the environment without the help of home, neighbors, or social institutions.

Meston's comprehension of the genre was poignantly demonstrated in "Pucket's New Year," televised January 5, 1957, but produced originally on the radio version of *Gunsmoke* on January 1, 1956. The story concerned Marshal Dillon's rescue of an old buffalo hunter named Pucket who had been shot and robbed by a partner, then left to die on the winter prairie. A fiercely independent, if slighty ignoble savage, Pucket balked at the thought of a doctor's care, even though his life was saved only by skillful amputation of much of his infected foot. Further, the prospect of settling permanently inside the protective town ran against the grain of this man from nature. After threats and bouts of depression, Pucket hatched a scheme to escape Dodge City by robbing the bank.

Dillon had little difficulty thwarting the old man's plan. With the would-be thief still in the bank, the marshal merely drove off the horse and wagon that Pucket had readied for an escape. More formidable a challenge, however, was the taming of Pucket's feral instincts and the conversion of this antisocial man to useful citizenship. Dillon accomplished this by dropping the robbery charges and arranging for Pucket's employment as a "shotgun" on the stagecoach, himself now guarding against possible robbery.

It was a masterful tale of the domestication of a wild man. It was Dillon's concern for human life that rescued Pucket, a wounded animal, from the unmerciful wilderness. It was a civilized doctor's medicine that saved his life. Although crippled and apprehensive, it was the rational process of town life to which Pucket physically and emotionally had to submit or perish.

Ironically, the decision to make the old man an armed guard gave him major responsibility for protecting the stagecoach as it traveled through the inhospitable wilds transporting citizens and goods between isolated pockets of civilazation. The brutal instinct of Pucket, a lame old churl from the anarchy of the wastelands, was now civilized and in the service of socialized humanity.

Whether juvenile or adult in its orientation, the Western was a staple of television programming for more than two decades. As regular a video offering as situation comedy or the detective story, the Western had roots deep in the national past and its TV manifestation seemed only a logical function of timelessness.

Yet the genre did not survive. In fact, the Western by the 1980s had practically disappeared from prime-time network TV. Where once a quarter of all evening first-run programming had been cowboy dramas, such offerings on television ceased to be viable popular culture. It was an unexpected outcome. Except for war series, which did not enjoy overwhelming popularity, never in television had a genre collapsed so completely. Yet the history of the Western from the mid-1960s to the present strongly indicates that the genre is lifeless—and in that passing are important implications for modern American political, social, and cultural thinking.

NOTES

1. For a history of the evolution of Marlboro's advertising imagery, see *Advertising Age*, October 27, 1958, pp. 3, 110. For figures on cigarette advertising revenues on TV in 1961, see "Ominous Rumble from Overseas," *Television Magazine*, June 1962, p. 55.

2. *Variety*, April 10, 1968, p. 42. Christopher Wicking and Tise Vahimagi, *The American Vein. Directors and Directions in Television* (New York: Dutton, 1979).

3. Johnny Mack Brown's comments are in James Horwitz, *They Went Thataway* (New York: Ballantine Books, 1978), pp. 141-42.

4. John Lardner, "The Hybrid Western," *The New Yorker*, January 18, 1958, p. 88; "The Hybrid Western (continued)," ibid., January 25, 1958, pp. 64-68; "Decline and Fall Possible," ibid., February 28, 1959, p. 97.

5. Clint Walker, "Foreword" to "Meanwhile Back at the Ranch" in *Who's Who in Television and Radio* I:6 (1955), p. 60. For an early scholarly discussion of the emergence of adult Westerns on TV, see Donald Howe Kirkley, Jr., "A Descriptive History of the Network Television Western during the Seasons 1955-56—1962-63," Ph.D. dissertation, Ohio University, 1967, pp. 102-30.

6. Cleveland Amory, "Review: The Dakotas," *TV Guide*, April 6, 1963, p. 1.

7. *TV Guide*, May 2, 1959, p. 11.

8. Eunice Field, "Wanted—Very Much Alive," *TV Radio Mirror*, April 1959, p. 61.

9. *TV Guide*, July 25, 1959, p. 19.

10. *TV Guide*, February 21, 1959, p. 13.

11. *TV Guide*, March 31, 1956, p. 7.

12. Richard A. R. Pinkham to Thomas McAvity, April 12, 1955. NBC Records, box 376, folder 18. For Miner's later assessment of why *Frontier* perished, especially his conclusion that NBC management acted too swiftly and too stupidly in canceling this anthology series, see Worthington Miner, *Worthington Miner* (Metuchen, N.J.: Scarecrow Press, 1985), pp. 248-50.

13. J. Fred MacDonald, *Don't Touch That Dial! Radio Programming in American Life, 1920-1960*, (Chicago: Nelson-Hall, 1979), pp. 195-229.

14. *Billboard*, October 28, 1957, p. 2.

15. *Variety*, November 27, 1957, p. 38.

16. John Reddy, "TV Westerns: The Shots Heard Round the World," *Reader's Digest*, January 1959, p. 136.

17. Todd Gitlin, *Inside Prime Time* (New York: Pantheon Books, 1983), p. 78.

18. John G. Cawelti, *The Six-Gun Mystique*, 2nd ed. (Bowling Green, Ohio: Popular Press, 1984), p. 94. Lardner, "Decline and Fall Possible," p. 97.

19. *Variety*, December 24, 1958, pp. 17, 30. *Maverick* also parodied other Western series. "Gun-shy" (January 11, 1959) was a satire of *Gunsmoke*; "Three Queens Full" (November 12, 1961) lampooned *Bonanza*; and "Hadley's Hunters" (September 25, 1960) spoofed all Warner Brothers video Westerns when Bart Maverick encountered the decidedly more stouthearted heroes of *Sugarfoot, Cheyenne, Bronco,* and *Lawman*.

20. *New York Times*, September 1, 1957, sec. 2, p. 13. A less profound assessment came from Pat Conway—who portrayed Sheriff Clay Hollister on *Tombstone Territory*—who boasted of Richard Dorso's series, "it's not a pseudo-arty, 'adult-type' Western. We're all proud of its being one series that takes the cowboy off the couch and puts him back on the horse where he belongs." Pat Conway, "How I Came to 'Tombstone Territory,'" in *The Television Annual for 1959*, Kenneth Baily, ed. (London: Odhams Press, 1958), p. 81.

21. Frank Gruber, "The 7 Ways to Plot a Western," *TV Guide*, August 30, 1958, pp. 5-7. See also Frank Gruber, *The Pulp Jungle*. (Los Angeles: Sherbourne Press, 1967), pp. 184-86. For several other analytical categories of the Western, see Philip French, *Westerns. Aspects of a Movie Genre*. (New York: Viking Press, 1973). p. 18.

22. *TV Guide*, October 22, 1960, pp. 28-29.

23. *Variety*, June 4, 1958, p. 46.

24. Leon Morse, "Hubbell Robinson Evaluates TV Programming Today," *Television Magazine*, December 1959, p. 50.

25. Ibid.

26. *Variety*, December 24, 1958, p. 17.

27. *TV Guide*, January 18, 1958, p. 29.

28. *Variety*, December 24, 1958, p. 17. See also Bob Johnson, "Why 'Maverick' Spurns the Code of the Western," *TV Guide*, August 1, 1959, pp. 17-19. In a booklet prepared by Huggins, "A Ten Point Guide to Happiness While Writing or Directing a *Maverick*," Huggins explained the essence of the brothers:

1. Maverick is the original disorganization man.

2. Maverick's primary motivation is that ancient and most noble of motives: the profit motive.

3. Heavies in *Maverick* are always absolutely right; and they are always beloved to someone.

4. The cliche flourishes in the creative arts because the familiar gives a sense of comfort and security. Writers and directors of *Maverick* are requested to live dangerously.

5. Maverick's activities are seldom grandiose. To force him into magnificent speculations is to lose sight of his essential indolence.

6. The *Maverick* series is a regeneration story in which the regeneration has been indefinitely postponed.

7. Maverick's travels are never aimless. He always has an objective in view: his pockets and yours. However, there are times when he is merely fleeing from heroic enterprise.

8. In the traditional western story the situation is always serious but never hopeless. In a *Maverick* story the situation is always hopeless but never serious.

9. 'Cowardly' would be too strong a word to apply to Maverick. 'Cautious' is possibly more accurate and certainly more kindly. When the two brothers went off to the Civil War their old pappy said to them, 'If either of you comes back with a medal I'll beat you to death.' They never shamed him.

10. The widely held belief that Maverick is a gambler is a fallacy. In his hands poker is not a game of chance. He plays it earnestly, patiently and with an abiding faith in the laws of probability." Cited in Marion Hargrove, "This Is a Television Cowboy?," *Life*, January 19, 1959, p. 75.

29. Bill Kelsay, "Clu Gulager," *TV Radio Mirror*, December 1960, p. 68.

30. Dwight Whitney, "Why 'Gunsmoke' Keeps Blazing," *TV Guide*, December 6, 1958, p. 11.

31. Dwight Whitney, "What's *Gunsmoke*'s Secret?," *TV Guide*, August 22, 1970, p. 24.

32. *Variety*, March 1, 1961, pp. 23, 70.

33. Dwight Whitney, "The Taming of the West—and *The Californians*—By Memo," *TV Guide*, September 13, 1958, p. 10.

34. *Variety*, September 11, 1957, p. 33.

35. *TV Guide*, November 8, 1958, p. 23.

36. *TV Guide*, March 26, 1960, p. 22.

37. George Eels, "TV Western Craze," *Look*, June 24, 1958, p. 70.

38. Eunice Field, "How a Western Is Made," *TV Radio Mirror*, May 1959, pp. 45-47, 73.

39. For a fuller version of McCoy's views on the authentic West, see his autobiography, coauthored with his son Ronald McCoy, *Tim McCoy Remembers the West* (Garden City, N.Y.: Doubleday, 1977).

40. A. William Bluem, *Documentary in Television: Form—Function—Method* (New York: Hastings House, 1965), p. 159.

41. Horace Newcomb, *TV: The Most Popular Art* (Garden City, N.Y.: Doubleday, 1974), p. 82.

42. Robert P. Ellis, "The Appeal of the Western Movie Thriller," *America*, May 17, 1958, p. 229.

43. *TV Guide*, April 30, 1960, p. 25. Ralph Brauer, *The Horse, the Gun, and the Piece of Property. Changing Images of the TV Western* (Bowling Green, Ohio: Popular Press, 1975), p. 53. Maurine Remenih, "No Rings around Ringo," *TV Radio Mirror*, May 1960, p. 78.

44. *Variety*, October 8, 1958, p. 29.

45. Herbert L. Jacobson, "Cowboy, Pioneer and American Soldier," *Sight and Sound*, April-June 1953, p. 189.

46. *TV Guide*, June 25, 1960, p. 18.

47. Joe Morhaim, "Why *Gunsmoke*'s Amanda Blake, Jim Arness Won't Kiss," *TV Guide*, March 15, 1958, pp. 9-10. This exact wording of the Arness quotation is in some doubt. In another printed source he is quoted as saying:

> Look, a cowboy wasn't tied down to one place or one woman. When he got mad, he hauled off and slugged someone. When he found a bottle of red-eye, he got good and drunk. Nowadays, people just don't seem to have the intestinal fortitude to live the way they'd like. That's why they tune in on Westerns, to get a breather from stifling conformity. They don't want to see Matt Dillon—or any other lawman—come home and sweep the kitchen.

See Jeff McBride, "The Man Who Stole His Life," *TV Radio Mirror*, January 1964, p. 64.

48. *Hollywood Reporter*, October 3, 1960.

49. *Variety*, October 5, 1960, p. 35.

50. As cited in Garner Simmons, *Peckinpah: A Portrait in Montage* (Austin: University of Texas Press, 1982), pp. 21-35. For another opinion of modern scholarship on "The Westerner" and "Jeff," see Paul Seydor, *Peckinpah: The Western Films* (Urbana: University of Illinois Press, 1980), pp. 3-16.

51. For the story behind Ford's directing of this episode of *Wagon Train*, see *TV Guide*, November 19, 1960, pp. 5-7.

52. In the screen credits the performance of John Wayne—whose real name was Marion Michael Morrison—was credited to Michael Morris.

4
The Adult Western: The Demise

In the halcyon years of the adult Western, from the late 1950s until the mid-1960s, the genre projected a world of danger. Frontier robbers and killers were a threatening breed. Their brutalizing qualities affected gentle townspeople who seemed safe neither on the streets nor in their homes.

The Western also told of disruptive social forces more fundamental than evil individuals. Here base human passions such as ignorance, intolerance, greed, hate, jealousy, and revenge often wreaked disastrous effects upon pioneer settlements. The ignoring of civilized standards or the abdication of social responsibilities also destabilized life on the frontier. In addition, there were natural calamities—fire, storm, flood, drought, and the like—that on occasion undermined the harmony of Western existence. It was within these parameters that TV Western characters operated.

There was, however, a cultural imperative influencing the history of the video Western. For a series—not to mention a genre—to attain popularity with a national audience, it must be accepted by a sufficiently large number of viewers. Given the nature of popular entertainment in the United States where it is commercial, competitive, ephemeral, and necessarily "purchased" by an audience, for any form to endure the mass audience must find and continue to find meaning in its realizations. This is accomplished when a cultural product is able to relate significantly to the values, fantasies, aspirations, anxieties, self-conceptualizations and other prevailing attitudes shared by the audience/customers.

All this the TV Western has ceased to do. Today cowboy programs are nonexistent and the genre is dead. Western drama is an anachronism. Where children once thrilled to the adventures of Hopalong Cassidy and the Range Rider, a new generation has neither heard their names nor seen their video exploits. Where adult men and women once spent much of their evenings observing the moral confrontations of Paladin and Rowdy Yates and Hoss Cartwright, there now are no Westerns in prime-time network TV—and there has not been a truly successful new Western series in two decades.

If the genre is not dead, it is at least in a deep, paralytic coma; and it will require a miraculous recovery bordering on resurrection if it ever is to regain importance as a popular diversion. This is because the entertainment form has become culturally unimportant. Its inner qualities are no longer acceptable to the mass audience. Its mystique and symbolism are questioned. Its messages are incongruent with contemporary social realities. Its stories are unwelcome. Its politics are controversial.

Social thought in the United States has changed during the 40 years that television has been an affordable popular medium, but the Western has failed to make the transition. Hobbled by its dated frame of reference and weakened by excesses that are generic, the Western on television has become extinct—worse yet, it has become irrelevant.

Some have maintained that the Western still lives in urban police dramas like *Miami Vice* and *Hill Street Blues*, and in the technological heroics in such series as *Airwolf* and *Knight Rider*. It is suggested that because other genres have captured some of its style and social purpose, the Western continues to influence American entertainment. Larry Michie writing in *Variety* in 1976, for example, explained that "this is the era of the new western, the cop show."[1]

As alluring as it sounds, this argument is myopic. Michael Knight's talking automobile in *Knight Rider* is not the equivalent of Paladin's black stallion. Stringfellow Hawke in his supercharged helicopter in *Airwolf* is no Sky King. The seedy criminality resolved weekly by Sonny Crockett and Rico Tubbs on *Miami Vice* does not equate to the outlawry handled by Wyatt Earp or the Lone Ranger. *Dragnet, The Lineup, The Naked City, Peter Gunn*, and other urban detective series flourished in the 1950s and early 1960s without being confused with Westerns. Even while the Western was in its prime, TV offered programs showing heroes other than cowboys entering the lives of troubled people, solving problems, then moving on to the next case —it was a medical calling on *Ben Casey*, on *Perry Mason* it was done for a fee, and on *Route 66* the service was performed free of charge.

The Western must be understood within a distinct set of criteria. This does not mean that these qualifiers exist exclusively for this genre. Some themes of the Western have been co-opted by other cultural forms. Aspects of its social relevance can be found in the detective story, the police procedural, modern adventure series, science fiction, and even situation comedy. But the totality of these criteria exists only in the Western and no amount of rhetoric can make Capt. Frank Furillo (of *Hill Street Blues*) into Marshal Matt Dillon.

The demise of the Western was not a quick development. Even during its glory years it exhibited signs of serious disorder. This was most obvious in the debilitating critique of the genre as inherently violent programming deleterious to public health, and in the first great compromise with its virility, the emergence of the domesticated Western.

VIOLENCE AND THE ATTACK UPON THE WESTERN

Criticism of the popular arts as glorifiers of violence—and the mass media as vehicles for popularizing, especially to youngsters, destructive images of brutality and criminality—was not new to television. However, as an entertainment medium that captured the mass audience with unprecedented quickness and finality, TV was especially vulnerable to scrutiny of its effects upon the national psyche.

From the beginning television executives faced a crescendoing critique of their product. Criticism came from individuals, organized groups, and government. One of the earliest complaints about video violence came from a private citizen in Chicago who in May 1949 purchased a full page in a local TV magazine to decry the unnerving imagery entering his home via the new medium. In the passionate tones that often have marked such assessments, this alarmed citizen wrote the following.

GRUESOME KILLINGS
IN OUR LIVING ROOMS
MUST BE STOPPED

We have a growing son. His little life is in the formative stage. Each day brings new thrills and experiences. He *does* what he sees and hears.

We can keep him away from public theaters, that have resorted to gruesome killings to attract blood-thirsty crowds (as in the old Roman gladiator days) but we cannot keep our son out of our own living room.

These stabbings, shootings, hangings, and killings must be kept out of our homes.

Television is still in the formative stage, the same as our own son. Help us keep television respectable—so we can try and raise a respectable citizen.

This full page ad of appeal is being paid for by one man, but one man is helpless in this undertaking. I need your help.

Write your U.S. congressman and send me a copy. Let's get the ball rolling to try and stop our children from murdering each other.[2]

From a single voice at the start, the attack on TV violence grew rapidly to national proportions. By 1965 an interim report of the U.S. Senate Juvenile Delinquency Subcommittee, chaired by Senator Thomas J. Dodd, came to conclusions more eloquently stated, but essentially the same, as those of that lone protester in Chicago. According to that interim report,

it is clear that television, whose impact on the public mind is equal to or greater than that of any other medium, is a factor in molding the character, attitudes, and behavior patterns of America's young people. Further, it is the subcommittee's view that the excessive amount of televised crime, violence, and brutality can and does contribute to the development of attitudes and actions in many young people which pave the way for delinquent behavior.[3]

From the beginning the violence permeating TV Westerns was a favorite target of protesters. Whether it was a critique by behavioral researchers, the Parent-Teachers Association, the U.S. Surgeon General, the U.S. Senate, city governmental agencies, religious task forces, or similar study groups, the Western—so attractive to children and so prevalent on television—was singled out as a major contributor to juvenile delinquency, a brutalizing reflection of a violence-prone society, an offender of civilized values.

It is important to note that television executives were sensitive to such public debate. As early as 1955 officials at NBC formalized rules regarding excessive violence in Westerns. This was done, according to Stockton Helffrich, the network's continuity acceptance director, "in response to parental concern and child-specialist suggestion that the cumulative effect of too-casual fatalities, of justice by six-gun rather than by more civilized processes, and of invariable exploitation of saloon locales and English-garbling protagonists might be damaging."[4]

Self-censorship was one matter; however, network concern was heightened when the chairman of the Federal Communications Commission (FCC) openly attacked the TV Western as banal and violent, a discredit to the industry and a disservice to the United States in the way it projected the American image abroad. This happened when Newton N. Minow, recently appointed by President John F. Kennedy to head the FCC, assailed the "vast wasteland" created by network television. Speaking on May 9, 1961, before a convention of the National Association of Broadcasters, Minow not only blasted TV for offering a "procession of . . . violence, sadism, murder, western badmen, western good men," but he wondered aloud:

> What will the people of other countries think of us when they see our Western badmen and good men punching each other in the jaw in between the shooting? What will the Latin American or African child learn of America from our great communications industry? We cannot permit television in its present form to be our voice overseas.

Minow was most unnerving, however, when he threatened to fight the license renewals of those who continued to air such "bad" television. "I understand that many people feel that in the past licenses were often renewed *pro forma*," he stated. "I say to you now: renewal will not be *pro forma* in the future. There is nothing permanent or sacred about a broadcast license."[5]

It is difficult to pinpoint the ways in which TV executives were influenced specifically by the Minow critique, or more generally by the years of public protest against TV violence. Television is, after all, a business and corporations do not readily make public their thinking on important decisions. There was at NBC, however, a deep division over the function and importance of violence in Western programming. The availability of several NBC letters and reports from the late 1950s and early 1960s now make it possible to document that controversy at least at one network.

In 1957 a researcher for NBC argued that the more violent programs lacked plausibility with viewers. "We live today in a social climate in which there is considerable respect—on the American scene —for the value of a man's life," wrote Dr. William J. Millard, Jr. in analyzing the forthcoming series, *Tales of Wells Fargo*. "The greater the number of lives snuffed out in a play," he continued, "the less apparent in the play is the standard of values by which we live from day to day. The more removed, therefore, it may be from what Americans sense to be the 'real' world."[6]

The other side of the argument was articulated in a letter written August 15, 1957, by Cyril C. Wagner, an NBC account executive, to an advertising agency interested in cosponsoring for Edsel automobiles the upcoming *Wagon Train* series. Wagner argued the case for violence in Western programming, claiming that "with any type of TV adventure program you naturally have to have some blood and thunder—that is what the public, and men particularly, want, as evidence[d] by audience rating records."[7]

While these documents offer insight into network ambivalence over Western violence, it is clear that those opposing aggressive representation were losing the debate. This became most apparent in a lengthy and revealing letter written July 13, 1961, by David Levy—the outgoing NBC vice-president in charge of TV programs and talent —to Robert W. Sarnoff, chairman of the board of NBC.[8] In 74 frank pages Levy sought to explain his accomplishments and to express frustration and dismay at being terminated by the network.

Levy was particularly sensitive to the speech delivered two months earlier by FCC chairman Minow blasting American television for its violence and banality.[9] Pointedly, Levy wrote of the failures of network and production company executives to diminish violence on television. He noted that his own official concern about TV violence had been stated as early as July 1960.

Levy reviewed his ongoing argument with network president Robert Kintner who "repeatedly emphasized the need for these elements [sex and violence] in the program structure of 1960-61." He explained a recent trip to Hollywood as emanating *out of my own conviction that violence must be curbed and not at anyone else's urging. I planned it, and made it, many weeks before Mr. Minow's famous speech*" [Levy's emphasis].

Levy was most specific with reference to Westerns on NBC that season. He reiterated his dismay with *Whispering Smith*, a series he originally felt to be "too violent" to schedule, only to be overruled by Kintner. Levy quoted an earlier letter he wrote criticizing the violence in an episode of *Bonanza*. Here he had cynically remarked, "If Adam [Cartwright] kills two men in his first show, by the end of the year the combined slaughter of four Cartwrights would be pretty impressive."

Levy also drew from his earlier memos expressing distaste for the level of violence in *The Tall Man* and *The Deputy*. He mentioned having personally discussed his ideas on video violence with the producers of *Tales of Wells Fargo, Wagon Train, The Outlaws, Bonanza, Laramie,* and *The Tall Man*.

Levy was a would-be network reformer who lacked the base of power from which to enforce his will. All he could do was attempt to persuade. This was apparent in his letter of May 17, 1961–a week after Minow's denunciation of TV violence–written to John Champion, the producer of *Laramie*.

> Last night I watched the episode of LARAMIE titled "Trigger Point." In the light of the recent visit I made to the coast . . . I think it important to point out that this particular episode was needlessly violent, and I would like to be specific.
>
> There were five killings, and in my judgment the impact of the show would not have been lessened at all if the number of killings had been reduced to three. For example, the old man could have been wounded and Robert Fuller could have brought him into town. In the showdown with the last of the outlaws Fuller in an aside to a townsman says, "Get a doctor." He comes into the saloon with both guns drawn and the last of the outlaws is killed. Here, too, in my judgment, it seems restraint could have been exercised and the outlaw could have been wounded and taken away by the doctor and a sheriff.
>
> I don't doubt that the episode passed through all normal channels of NBC but I submit that it is exactly the kind of unnecessary violence that will not pass the coming season.
>
> I believe that we should do everything possible to reduce "shootouts," killings and unnecessary violence. I would also like to urge you to eliminate excessive drinking.
>
> I believe that on reflection and with greater creative effort on the part of writers and greater supervision on your part the stories on LARAMIE can be exactly as Western without subjecting you or us to justifiable criticism.

THE DOMESTIC WESTERN

Despite the departure of sensitive programmers like David Levy, there were major changes emerging in the TV Western by the mid-1960s. The genre on TV was experiencing a deemphasis of violence. Fights and killings would continue to occur, but by the end of the decade dramatic savagery was waning. Academicians like George Gerbner of the Annenberg School of Communications of the University of Pennsylvania could report that in the period 1967-69 those involved in violence in prime-time drama, either as victims or violators, dropped from 73 percent to 64 percent; that in comic situations the figure fell from 22 percent to 14 percent; and that the weekly casualty list fell from 437 in 1967 to 134 in 1969, and from 182 violent deaths in 1967 to 46 dead per week in 1969.[10] Certainly such moderation resulted in part from chronic popular criticism, as well as attacks from influential leaders such as the chairman of the FCC; but it also seems to have been influenced by the shifting tastes of the mass audience.

As a society given to commercial crazes—or socialized to consume in those periodic bursts of purchasing enthusiasm that are the bases of such waves of popularity—more than five years of cowboy dramas had satisfied much of the mass appetite for the genre. This was noticeable in a general decline in ratings for Westerns throughout the 1960s. It was reflected further in the failure rate for new cowboy series. Between 1965 and 1968, for example, there were 21 Westerns introduced in the fall seasons. Of that number only 4 lasted more than two years —13 failed in one season or less; 1 lasted a season and one-half; and 3 finished their second seasons before being canceled. Significantly, no new Westerns were offered in the fall of 1969.

The most significant indicator of the change in popular tastes, however, was evidenced in the domestication of the genre—and in its modified product, the domestic Western. While most adult cowboy dramas dealt with law officers and wandering do-gooders, this type of Western was based upon family life. Such series usually focused on sprawling cattle empires or other grand enterprises maintained by rugged individualists. In programs usually running 60 or 90 minutes these offerings depicted respectable men and women with democratic values, pioneering types who honorably fought natural and human adversities in order to thrive in the West. Importantly, too, this domestic variety was the only type of Western to survive in the late 1960s and into the following decade.

Faced with a diversity of challenges to life, property, and civilized standards, families in domestic Westerns came together weekly to fight for their frontier existences. Certainly this theme was not unfamiliar in literature and motion pictures. Moreover, television Westerns emphasizing family ties had appeared in the late 1950s at a time when the more rugged style was at its peak. Beginning with programs like *The Rifleman* in 1958, where Lucas McCain frequently lectured his young son on the facts of social responsibility, or even the short-lived *Buckskin*, which the same year featured a widow boardinghouse-keeper and her ten-year-old son facing life in pioneer Montana, homey feelings were integrated into the adult genre.

By the mid-1960s, however, the only Westerns popular on TV were those offering families or family-like units in contests with a range of antagonists. Typically, in *The High Chaparral* the Cannon family and its employees fought to keep their large ranch viable in the Arizona desert near Tucson. In lusher surroundings *Lancer* concerned a cattle and timber empire in the San Joaquin Valley of California, a 100,000-acre ranch headed by widower Murdoch Lancer, his two quarrelsome sons, and a young female ward. More austere was the Kansas homestead owned, operated, and defended by the Pride family in *The Road West*.

By its themes and characterizations, the domestic Western represented a modification of the lone-rider heroics so recognizable in most early adult cowboy dramas. Such change was best epitomized in *The Big Valley*. Set in the San Joaquin Valley of central California, this series was headed by a woman. Matriarchy was not unknown in the real West, but in the video West women were almost always subordinate to men. After all, the Western was a masculine genre, and the principal audience for the TV Western was male. Thus the appearance of Barbara Stanwyck as strong-willed Victoria Barkley, ruler of the vast Barkley ranch, was unprecedented. Moreover, assisted in the enterprise by a daughter and three rugged sons, Victoria Barkley made *The Big Valley* a popular offering, enduring four seasons and 111 hour-long installments.

The domestic Western covered a wide chronological and geographical range. *Daniel Boone* dealt with the historic Boone living with his family in backwoods Kentucky in the late eighteenth century. Set in the 1960s, *Empire* (later called *Redigo*) featured the Garrett family ranch in Santa Fe and those who dealt with its welfare in the modern West.

The ruggedness of Wyoming was a favorite locale for several domestic Westerns. *The Virginian* (later called *The Men from Shiloh*) concerned the folks who owned and operated the Shiloh ranch near Medicine Bow. *Laramie*, an early domestic Western that ended its run in late 1963, concerned two friends who owned a combination cattle ranch and stagecoach depot in the 1880s. In a twist on such series, *The Monroes* treated the five recently orphaned Monroe children—pioneer immigrants from Illinois and aged from 18 to 6 years—trying to maintain their parents' Teton valley homestead against assorted challenges.

Wherever or whenever they were situated, domestic Westerns spoke of land and home and close social relationships, themes well understood by most viewers. The Western may have thrived when it depicted gun fights and heroes who rode in from the mountains or prairies to bring peace to the valley, but by the end of the 1960s American audiences responded best to stories underscoring family units acting together. Such representations extended from the action in "The Great Safe Robbery"—an episode of *The Big Valley* aired November 21, 1966, in which Victoria Barkley and her daughter were kidnapped by bank robbers but eventually rescued by the three Barkley brothers—to the sentimentalism expressed in "A Love to Remember"—an episode of *The Virginian* aired October 29, 1969, wherein the Virginian expressed to his sweetheart his deepest feelings on the meaning of life in the West.

> Girl: Tell me more about it—that place you're going to build some-day.
>
> Virginian: [It's] in Wyoming country. The river runs through there, called the Sweetwater—snows some in the winter. But in the spring the whole valley comes up green. Man could get a coupla sections pretty cheap. Start a herd—even a family, maybe.
>
> Girl: In that order?
>
> Virginian: Well, that all depends. You start a herd all by yourself. My understanding's that a family takes a certain amount of co-operation.
>
> Girl: Seems to me I've heard that myself.
>
> Virginian: Tell you this though—be a fine place to watch a bunch of kids grow up.
>
> Girl: I can see it: big old house on a hill, and beams in the living room, and a great stone fireplace with a bearskin rug in front of it. And trees, oak trees all around.
>
> Virginian: That's funny. I did kinda have a spot picked out for the house. It's on a hill. There's a good stand of oak up there, too. How'd you guess that?

At a time when video violence was under fire from citizens and government, the domestic Western offered an antidote. Its reliance upon sentimentality often meant the downplaying of violent conflict. With families sitting around dinner tables or visiting town together, there was less opportunity for brutal conflict. Thus, while a rugged series like *Lancer* occasionally offered a fast-draw confrontation or a he-man fight over a lady, it tended to accentuate deeper themes such as the story of the growing love between an orphaned child entertainer and her emotionally reserved spinster aunt in "Little Darling of the Sierras" (November 18, 1969); or the O. Henryesque tale of the Lancer men selflessly giving treasured possessions to neighbors needier than themselves in "The Gifts" (October 28, 1969).

The domestic Western that most successfully showed the pioneer family in combat with frontier adversities was *Bonanza*. In fact, this series pioneered the programming style. For 10 of its almost 14 seasons on NBC, it was rated among the top ten TV attractions. Furthermore, for three consecutive years, 1964-67, it was the most watched series in the nation.

Bonanza told of the Cartwright family—a widower and his three sons—and its experiences operating the Ponderosa ranch, a timberland and cattle empire in the Comstock Lode country in and around Virginia City, Nevada. Blending action, dramatic characterization, and human interest plots, *Bonanza* projected a family that was strong yet emotionally sensitive. As its patriarch, Ben Cartwright was a tough, rational pioneer whose honesty and civic instincts were reflected in his sons: the intense Adam, the physically strong but spiritually gentle Hoss, and the impetuous Little Joe.

The sense of family love and struggle for the common good so essential to the domestic Western was well described in the publicity kit that accompanied syndicated *Bonanza* programs:

> The sight of the Cartwrights charging down a hillside on horseback—Old Ben with his great mane of hair whipping behind him like a Biblical prophet; Adam, with the deadly eyes of a swooping hawk; Hoss, so huge of chest and shoulder that the giant bay under him looked puny by comparison; and Little Joe, a wild rebel yell on his lips—was enough to cow the coolest man. And this close-knit family of men stood between the silver barons and the most extensive stretch of timberland in the Comstock Lode area.
>
> The Cartwrights controlled the vast Ponderosa, a ranch that extended from the lush shores of Lake Tahoe down the snow-capped slopes of the Sierras and east to the desert-like environs of Virginia City. Over part of its thousand square miles roamed 10,000 head of cattle, grazing in the grassy lowlands; the rest of the acreage was covered with thickly wooded hills, studded with magnificient evergreens.
>
> The job of patrolling and protecting their holdings, of guarding the treasured territory against cattle rustlers and timber raiders, was a task calling for the utmost vigilance and bravery, the sharpest eyes and the surest aim. The Cartwrights possessed these qualities and more. Woe to the stranger who set foot on their land. Dozens of dead could testify to the futility of expeditions organized to take over the Ponderosa. But the Cartwrights knew the mining tycoons would never give up trying. They and their adversaries also knew that as long as they were together, the Cartwrights would never be beaten.

While *Bonanza* stories revolved about the family unit as it battled for survival against jealous rivals, the series emphasized human concern and charity. If in concept the family was the primary social unit of mutual support and shared love, *Bonanza* accentuated the fact that even in times of great challenge, humane interests were critical to lasting, effective social values. Typically, in "Pursued" (October 2 and 9, 1966) the Cartwrights endured local antagonism to offer sanctuary and medical assistance to a Mormon family being harassed by local religious bigots. In "My Brother's Keeper" (April 7, 1963), brotherly love was at issue in Adam's disgust with frontier life, an emotion he openly expressed after accidentally shooting Little Joe. In "A Dream to Dream" (April 14, 1968), Hoss interceded in a family dispute, rescuing a woman and her two children from an abusive, alcoholic husband.

By the end of the decade only two Westerns enjoyed sizable followings: the domestic *Bonanza* and the more traditional *Gunsmoke*. In the case of *Gunsmoke*, however, its longevity was directly related to the ability of its producers to bring to the series the spirit of the domestic Western.

In *Gunsmoke* the family was implied. After years together, Matt, Kitty, Doc, Chester, Festus, and other secondary characters made Dodge City the residence for a family of interactive frontier types who chose to abide by the law and to oppose together those who broke it. In an interview in 1985, William Blinn—who wrote for *Gunsmoke* in the late 1960s—explained the familial qualities of the series.

> Certainly, there have been very few shows that created an on-camera family as well as they did without having any blood ties. But between Matt and Doc and Festus and Chester, when he was there—I mean there was an ensemble feeling of caring and interrelationships and interconnectiveness. I wish I had friends like that. I wish all my relationships were as nondevious and nonmanipulative as these were because they were a classic extended family.[11]

Interestingly, *Gunsmoke* lasted eight extra seasons because it was able to make the transition to the relevant characterization that marked the domestic Western. In fact, by 1967 its ratings had collapsed so severely it was canceled by CBS. Only the personal intervention of network president William S. Paley rescued the series. A change of time slots, an emphasis upon relevant human drama, and the introduction of a young new character, the handsome gunsmith Newly O'Brien, revived its popularity. As evident in Table 9, changes by the fall of 1967 had startling results almost immediately for the series.

It is significant that *Gunsmoke* continued to thrive into the 1970s precisely because it developed the type of humanistic flavor found in the success of *Bonanza*. Aired Mondays at 7:30 P.M. (EST), *Gunsmoke* reached a new and younger audience than the graying viewer-

Table 9 *Gunsmoke* **Ratings History, 1955-75**

Season	Rank	Average Rating	Average Share	Average Audience (in millions)
1955-56	*	*	*	*
1956-57	8	32.7	*	*
1957-58	1	43.1	*	*
1958-59	1	39.6	60	*
1959-60	1	40.3	64.6	*
1960-61	1	37.3	62.2	17,244
1961-62	3	28.3	47.3	13,594
1962-63	10	27.0	45.6	13,424
1963-64	20	23.5	39.5	12,030
1964-65	27	22.6	38.1	11,890
1965-66	30	21.3	37.4	11,460
1966-67	34	19.9	34.8	10,930
1967-68	4	25.5	40.3	14,280
1968-69	6	24.9	38.0	14,190
1969-70	2	25.9	39.0	15,330
1970-71	5	25.5	39.0	15,330
1971-72	4	26.0	39.0	16,150
1972-73	8	23.6	35.0	15,290
1973-74	15	22.1	33.0	14,630
1974-75	26**	20.7	*	*

*Figures not available.
**Indicates tie.
Source: Statistics courtesy of A. C. Nielsen Company, Northbrook, Illinois.

ship it maintained during its first 12 years on Saturday nights at 10 P.M. (EST). Now the series highlighted matters that related to the concerns of its fresh viewership. Here were stories concerning children and young adults; and family themes were accentuated, be it Festus visiting his hillfolk kin ("Hard-Luck Henry" aired October 23, 1967), Doc Adams seeking a home for newly born orphaned triplets ("Baker's Dozen" aired December 25, 1967), or Matt Dillon rescuing his "family"—Newly, Doc, Kitty, and Festus—from murderous bounty hunters ("The Long Night" aired February 17, 1969).

The towering heroics of Matt Dillon softened as the series developed loyalties with a younger audience, itself affected by profound reevaluations underway in the United States in the late 1960s. The revived *Gunsmoke* might involve blacks or Hispanics or Indians in a drama about racial prejudice, or the military might be the target of a story critical of institutional biases. While *Gunsmoke* was always a morality play, according to producer John Mantley in 1970, "the morality of 15 years ago was too simple and basic. You can't get away with that today."[12]

Domestic Westerns had staying power. Into the 1960s, as governmental and private pressure groups increasingly assailed the genre for excessive displays of violence, most of the more forceful series were canceled. The domestic programs, however, enjoyed lengthy runs. While the glamorous photography of a series like *Cimarron Strip*, or the action in *Custer* or *Hondo* or *The Dakotas* found no widespread acceptance, several domestic Westerns endured for years—and for many more years as syndicated reruns.

By the end of the decade, it was clear that only as a vehicle demonstrating familial themes was the genre viable on television. Even by this date, however, except for *Gunsmoke* and *Bonanza*, few TV cowboy series remained. As Les Brown explained it in *Variety* in early 1969—under the front-page banner headline, "TV Westerns Bite the Dust"—the genre was approaching extinction.

> A little gunplay, a fist in the gut, an occasional trampling in the stampede, a saloon brawl, a ranch on fire, a kick in the ribs, a ride or a fall off a cliff—these have been the lifeblood of the classic American morality tale, and now they're no longer considered civilized.

In explaining this cultural collapse Brown inculpated the most chronic critics of television: "The militants against violence have shot down the tv cowboy."[13]

It is simplistic to conclude that persistent criticism of violence, even from powerful people and institutions, eventually destroyed the video Western. Certainly there was a diminishing of TV violence as measured in the late 1960s. That this trend paralleled the ascendancy of domestic Westerns and the demise of more aggressive cowboy dramas is obvious.

However, when the Western was gone from television, violence reappeared. As late as November 1984 one interest group, the National Coalition on TV Violence, could claim that video violence had risen 75 percent since 1980 and was now at record levels.[14] While violence returned to TV with a vengeance, the Western was unable to regain its position in network television.

Furthermore, if one accepts the boundaries of violence described by Dr. Rose K. Goldsen, it seems clear that the Western was not the only TV genre to assault popular sensibilities with murder and mayhem—yet only the Western perished.

> What kind of violence? Physical violence, emotional violence, violence to bodily integrity, violence to sense of self, violence by direct contact, violence by remote control, violence to one's peers, violence to one's superiors, violence by authority figures, violence by the powerful, violence by the deviant, violence by the frustrated, violence as a norm, violence as pathological behavior, violence for vengeance, violence to correct miscarriage of justice, violence by men to men, men to women, women to women, women to men, violence about sex, violence in sex, violence by animals or involving animals, violence by children or to children, violence whose consequences are shown, violence whose consequences are inferred, violence that is justified, violence in a measure appropriate to some previous injury, face-to-face acts of violence, institutional violence, violence in war . . . I could go on.[15]

The genre died for reasons other than its violence. Had it waned simply because audience appetite for cowboy shows had been glutted, according to the cyclical pattern noticeable in all TV programming, its return should be predictable; but it never returned to popularity. While there were Western series introduced in the 1970s and 1980s, they have been dismal failures. That being the case, the death of the Western must be sought elsewhere.

The television Western, even in its most violent manifestations, flourished because it meshed harmoniously with widely accepted social and political views of its times. If it is no longer viable, the reasons for its fall must be related to fundamental sociopolitical changes that render the genre obsolete. The roots of these basic shifts are found in the reevaluations in popular thinking that began in the 1960s. To understand this relationship between the viability of an entertainment form and the development of popular thought, it first is necessary to consider the TV Western in terms of the principal motifs through which it related to an American audience.

THE WESTERN AS LEGAL DRAMA

Above all, central characters understood their activities in terms of the law. Law was at the foundation of the civilization they protected. Without law there was no order or process, no purpose, no society. Conversely, the certainty in the law they upheld created credible, emulable champions.

In the view of scholars Horace Newcomb and Robert S. Alley the Western—as "America's primary story of social authority, of the legitimate and illegitimate uses of violence in the process of creating order, making civilization"—explained "our reasons for having rules in the first place."[16] However, Marshal Jim Crown phrased it more bluntly to a would-be lynch mob in "Broken Wing," an episode of *Cimarron Strip* television September 21, 1967.

> Now we ain't got much law around here. But what law we have we're gonna follow. You all can build a gallows in your own backyard—if you have a mind to and if you've got the lumber. There's only one that's gonna be used, if it's used. That's over in Ft. Smith. The man that uses it is gonna have a legalized death warrant in his hand. Now you can chew on that and swallow it, and we just might then get along.

The TV West was a place where good, legal men stopped obvious criminals. Extenuating circumstances might have elicited a degree of compassion from the viewing audience, but they never blunted the law enforcement process. Ultimately, the rudimentary civilization nurtured on the television frontier had to be saved from corruptive, evil people. Even those guilty by reason of insanity had to be captured, reformed, or killed.

Given the overwhelming popularity of the genre, viewers at this time apparently agreed with the actions taken by their champions. Measuring desperadoes against popularly accepted standards of right and wrong, solutions were forthcoming quickly and decisively. In its streamlined way, the TV Western communicated, and viewers endorsed, a smoothly functioning, if simplified system of social justice.

Yet, the video Western projected an interpretation of the American legal system that was perhaps misleading. The complexities so frustratingly a part of modern legal reality were absent in this facile television world. Lawyers were practically nonexistent; and where they did appear, they frequently were shown to be dishonest. Court technicalities like restraining orders, search warrants, plea bargains, and trial delays were absent. Instead, decisions were apparent and swift, and justice was always served within a 30-, 60-, or 90-minute time frame.

This was a seductive legality, offering direct and often definitive action as the answer to social problems. When Sheriff Clay Hollister encountered noisy troublemakers in *Tombstone Territory*, how right it seemed for him to throw the rowdies in jail. Other TV law officers might have required fisticuffs or the butt of a gun to quell the trouble-makers, but malcontents were eliminated and society returned to tranquility if only for the moment.

Citizen avengers and paralegal heroes learned well their lessons in direct action. When corporation investigator Jim Hardy on *Tales of Wells Fargo* or the mercenary Paladin on *Have Gun—Will Travel* had their lives threatened, how quick each was to draw and slay his op-pressor. At home and on the screen, moreover, few seemed to ques-tion the propriety of such a response. When the tranquility of the Lancer, Shiloh, or High Chaparral ranch was upset by outside forces, justified reactions by defenders of property rights and responsible social freedom ultimately resolved the dilemma. Even if such reac-tions involved killing, few at home seemed to denounce the need for such responsiveness—few apparently even wondered whatever hap-pened to the corpses of those shot down while operating outside the law.

This attitude was described by Robert Horton, a costar of *Wagon Train*, and later star of his own series, *A Man Called Shenandoah*. "The critics say there are too many dead bodies in *Wagon Train*," Horton explained in 1961. "If I'm going to be on next week's show, there must be dead bodies. In the period of history we're dealing with, it's either kill or be killed. Anybody who studies history knows that. . . ."[17]

The fine points of civil liberties and innocence-until-proven-guilty were not always applicable here. What the TV Western was offering was open warfare, a protracted battle between obvious legality and illegality. At stake was control of civilization. There was neither time nor reason for studied response. The answer to each dilemma was ob-vious: enough strategy, enough muscle, enough gunpowder. Through the concerted application of the brains and brawn of good men, this form of adult entertainment showed, indeed advocated, an efficient way to tame the savage and rescue humanity.

How well this legal philosophy was suited to a nation challenging civil rights illegalities at home while waging war abroad against illegal Communist aggression. At the beginning, both crusades seemed so right: black Americans deprived of their social rights needed heroes, champions who would ride into dangerous situations, rectify oppres-sive problems, then ride away after thwarting the representatives of injustice and reforming the rest of the citizenry.

In the Vietnam War the scenario was equally appropriate. The Western was a natural metaphor for this undeclared conflict. Here bad Reds from the North and their renegade cohorts in the South were violating standards of decency by seeking to dislodge a good government in Saigon. Like those selfless do-gooders in so many TV Westerns, brave American men were now risking life and limb to help the besieged innocents of the South who wanted nothing more than a little land, a little peace, a little democracy.[18]

Needless to say, neither the civil rights movement nor the Vietnam War continued to be so easily understood. There were so many compromising developments in the civil rights movement: white backlash hostile to social reforms for Afro-Americans; internal dissention, even murders, within the black movement; rebellions in the urban ghettos; the election of political leaders ready to manipulate and exploit white fears. What began as a crusade for the achievement of fundamental legal rights degenerated into confusion and fell short of its goal. The formulaic framework of Western legality no longer fit the litigious world emerging by the end of the 1960s. In a society of court-ordered busing, mandatory quotas, federal-state-local guidelines on affirmative action, forced integration of neighborhoods, and the like, many people decided that the bad guys in the movement were good and the good guys were bad. This was something that would never happen in a Western.

Similarly, the war in Southeast Asia soon lost its innocent, cowboy qualities. The noble self-sacrifice demanded eventually became socially disquieting. While many continued to ride to the rescue in Vietnam, there was a sizable contingency of doubters at home. Protest marches in the streets of the United States, the usage of narcotics by front-line U.S. troops in Vietnam, draft-card burners, clergymen protesting the war, dislike of the allied South Vietnamese troops, and the killing of U.S. officers by enlisted men in the field—these were not the hallmarks of Western-like military action. All of this developed in a conflict that legally did not exist since there never was a formal congressional declaration of war as prescribed by the U.S. Constitution.

THE WESTERN AS MORAL DRAMA

If the adult television Western proffered a seductive interpretation of the law and its enforcement, it also dealt with the religious and humanistic morality basic to American civilization. In fact, legality and morality were often synonymous. This was succinctly noted in

"Day of the Scorpion," an episode of *The Virginian* aired September 22, 1965. Here one character declared: "We have laws here, Mr. Pierce, to hold all of us in. . . . Law and morality have to be the same thing."

In this way Western heroes were moral as well as legal agents. In their actions were found ethical, even religious, judgments. Importantly, three of the more compelling contemporary explanations of the video Western suggested that the genre held great moral significance.

For Peter Homans in 1962, the Western was essentially "a Puritan morality tale in which the savior-hero redeems the community from the temptations of the devil." Certainly, all viewers did not consciously register such a metaphysical relationship each time Johnny Yuma on *The Rebel* or Clay Culhane on *Black Saddle* bested a criminal and saved a town. As a pattern of social action, however, the formula closely followed the fundamental motif of Christian faith—the single selfless savior giving his life for the salvation of the multitude.

In Homans's view the Western champion was a religious operative moving within a secular environment to reaffirm the Judeo-Christian morality originally planted in American civilization by Puritan ancestors. "Tall in the saddle," remarked Homans, the Western hero "rides straight from Plymouth Rock to a dusty frontier town" where "his Colt .45 is on the side of the angels."[19]

Two years earlier Martin Nussbaum delineated the sociological symbolism detectable in the adult Western, an important quality of which was the moral persuasiveness of the genre. According to him, the Western proposed that all men were both good and bad, but that by their own will or by unavoidable circumstances some "have placed themselves on the wrong side of the law, a law which transcends man's law and has overtones of moralistic law."

In this dilemma, according to Nussbaum, the Western hero operates as a decisive moral force. "It falls to the western hero, then, to judge the rightness and wrongness of an act and to satisfy the law if it has been violated." With reference to the contemporary social and political quandaries, he added: "Today when all our problems are so complicated that there really is no right or wrong but rather many shades of gray, it is gratifying to see complex problems reduced to an either-or proposition, adjudicated and resolved by a single action."[20]

More theological in its direction than either Nussbaum's or Homans's argument was the explanation offered in 1957 by Alexander Miller in *The Christian Century* magazine. Miller stressed the appearance within the genre of many of the profound dialectical themes of Christian theology. Pilgrimage and rest, justice and mercy, war and

peace—basic contradictions between which religious humanity fluctu-
ated—were integral to the TV Western as well as spirtuality.

Miller contended that the cowboy hero was a fatalistic, yet moralistic, individual. "A man does what he has to do," claimed Miller,
"and justifies it in one way or another." Like modern religious man,
the central character in the video Western possessed "the incorrigible
yearning after virtue, the inevitable implication in sin, the irrepressible
inclination to self-justification." He concluded that in the genre "every
theological theme is here, except the final theme, the deep and heal-
ing dimension of guilt and grace."[21]

Again, however, social realities since the 1960s have impinged
upon the uncomplicated moral vista proffered by the Western. The
generalized reformism of the past 20 years has created a moral ambivalence unanticipated in the genre. From civil rights and the Vietnam War, to the ecology movement and the crusade for women's
rights, new "good guys" and "bad guys" have been recognized. But if
good can change, and good equates to moral, where is the universal
morality so crucial to the Western? In a world of moral justice, there
is no place for the politics of Governor George C. Wallace, yet in the
late 1960s he found great national support, in part because of his
opposition to the black social movement. In a world of moral certi-
tude, there could be no simultaneous appreciation for Abby Hoffman
and General William C. Westmoreland. Yet both men—one a respected
leader in the anti-War movement, the other the most celebrated officer to emerge from the Vietnam conflict—had their moral constituencies. What to one group of women appeared as a "male chauvinist
pig," to another might be the stereotypical Western hero doing his
formulaic duty. What to some in the civil rights movement cynically
might be termed an "uncle Tom" faction, to others might appear rational, temperate, and distinguished. When labor unions oppose clean-
ing up the environment because it might cost jobs, where is the moral
right?

It might accomodate psychotic behavior, but the Western made
no provision for such moral confusion. Yet to remain accepted, the
genre had to fit into a society in flux. The reevaluations under way in
American thought since the mid-1960s clashed with the fundamental
certainties of the Western. The religious base of the genre described
by Homans and Miller might still be discernible, but the social answers
communicated by the Western heroes have been compromised. Erectly
they might have sat in their saddles as they rode from Plymouth Rock
to Dodge City and beyond, but the value systems they upheld were

no longer accepted unquestioningly by a sufficiently large component of the American population.

THE WESTERN AS POLITICAL DRAMA

The message of the adult Western meshed well with the political climate of the late 1950s and early 1960s. This was a time of international Cold War, and the Western inspired the nation. "It was no accident that the renaissance of the cowboy film took place during and immediately after World War II," wrote the British film scholar Herbert L. Jacobson in 1953. "And as America girds herself for the possibility of another great struggle," he continued, "it is not surprising that the frequency of these films, which reflect and nourish her picture of herself as a successful defender of high ideals, has been stepped up."[22]

In the popular American view of the time, this was a contest between good and evil. On one side appeared the Soviet Union as advocate of communism, crusher of hopes for global peace, brutal master of captured nations, would-be conqueror of the Earth. On the other side stood the selfless United States of America as advocate of freedom, protector of the downtrodden, champion of Free World democracy, proponent of bourgeois capitalism. The Russians were global outlaws: forcefully grabbing other people's countries, undermining world stability, threatening the future of mankind. Wanting nothing but freedom and happiness for everyone, however, the Americans hoped only to rescue the world for honest people—to thwart the expansionists and bring a happy conclusion to this challenge from godless Red "bad guys."

It seemed so easy to comprehend. Indeed, it was well understood by the citizens of the United States. Fearful of Soviet expansionism overseas and Red subterfuge at home, the once isolationist Americans slid deeply into a prepossessing rivalry with the Soviet enemy.

No one was unaffected. The Cold War was a pervasive reality. Like those innocent ranchers and townspeople in countless Westerns who found their parochial existences threatened by dastardly outlaws, unassuming Americans at this time of global tension were compelled to defend themselves, their possessions, and the values for which they stood. A noble cause had been thrust upon them. Failure to act heroically might have been tragic.

In the late 1960s Swedish film scholars Leif Furhammar and Folke Isaksson recognized this pattern when they wrote of the Western myth of silent, lonely men riding off the prairie to take up arms in noble defense of freedom-loving farmers against "gangs bent on grabbing land and money." "This national myth fitted the United States to perfection when the Truman doctrine against communist expansion was proclaimed," they contended. Furhammar and Folke even suggested that "the Western plot offers the perfect filter through which to look at the Vietnam war."[2 3]

The Western was the nation's most popular militaristic genre and its influence was apparent as the Cold War became hot and bloody in Southeast Asia. In his book *Backfire*—a perceptive analysis of historic cultural dispositions in the United States and their influential role in leading the American people into the Vietnam War—Loren Baritz has remarked on the prevalence in that conflict of the language and symbols of the Western. According to him, John Wayne became "a model and a standard" for an "astonishing" number of American soldiers in Vietnam. He continued, "Everyone in Vietnam called dangerous areas Indian country." Paraphrasing the familiar phrase, "The only good Indian is a dead Indian," Baritz added that "some GIs painted on their flak jackets THE ONLY GOOD GOOK IS A DEAD ONE. They called their Vietnamese scouts who defected from the Communists Kit Carsons."

Poignantly, Baritz described how U.S. soldiers in Vietnam often justified their activities in terms of the frontiersman logic learned through visual media.

> These nineteen-year-old Americans, brought up on World War II movies and westerns, walking through the jungle, armed to the teeth, searching for an invisible enemy who knew the wilderness better than they did, could hardly miss these connections. One after another said, at some point, something like, "Hey, this is just like a movie."[2 4]

Indeed, the young men fighting in Vietnam in the 1960s and 1970s were nurtured on the abundance of Westerns that had glutted television five to ten years earlier. This generation of warriors learned as children to define itself with reference to the cowboy imagery and rhetoric delivered so approvingly via TV. Moreover, this generation accepted the Western so overwhelmingly in part because its stories explained so much so easily.

In many ways the political-military-philosophical scenario of the Cold War was familiar to viewers of television cowboy dramas. The linkage between anti-Communist politics and the flourishing TV Western was aptly summarized by David Shea Teeple in *The American Mercury* magazine in 1958. Arguing against the diplomatic weakness of "dressed-up dude rancher" politicians, and in favor of the successful "rough and ready character," Teeple summoned a legion of television stalwarts to press his point.

> Would a Wyatt Earp stop at the 38th Parallel, Korea, when the rustlers were escaping with his herd? Ridiculous! Would a Marshal Dillon refuse to allow his deputies to use shotguns for their own defense because of the terrible nature of the weapon itself? Ha! Would the Lone Ranger, *under any circumstance*, allow himself to be bullied and threatened by those who sought to destroy the principles by which he lives? Would "Restless Gun" or Jim Hardy of "Wells Fargo" attempt to *buy* friends who would fight for the right? Can you imagine Paladin of "Have Gun Will Travel" standing aside, while women and children were being massacred? Can you imagine Cheyenne living in a perpetual state of jitters because he fears the next move of some gun slinger? Would Judge Roy Bean release a murderer on some technicality devised by a slick lawyer? Would Wild Bill Hickok sell guns to the badmen?[25]

Again, realities made painfully apparent since the 1960s have undermined the facile qualities of the political philosophy in the Western. A war against communism in Southeast Asia cost billions of U.S. dollars, more than 58,000 lives, and hundreds of thousands of physical and emotional wounds. A high price to pay, but when it resulted in military defeat and politically negligible advantage for the United States, popular thinking on militaristic enterprise was perforce affected.[26]

Furthermore, if the Western flourished because it mirrored popular thought in the Cold War, that period of U.S. history is not only completed, but the uncritical belief and unquestioning trust that characterized the time have been eroded. While contemporary politics still gives evidence of nationalistic fervor and intense rivalry with a communist enemy, these sentiments are neither as widespread nor as uncritically accepted as in the 1950s and 1960s. Where once it meshed perfectly with the fearful yet crusade-like temper of the Cold War era, the Western now must fit into a society of conflicting, articulated, and relatively informed political awareness. The inability of the Western to find a mass constituency in a society of relatively open debate is a testimony to the depth of the new social and political attitudes developed by many Americans during and after the Vietnam War.

THE WESTERN AND NATIONALISM

In the blending of legal, moral, and political self-justification that was the TV Western, millions throughout this period of unprecedented international tension saw nightly dramas about the triumphs of their forefathers over moral threats. From the adult TV format to vintage B feature films—movies whose spirit Johnny Mack Brown once described as "athletic and exciting and American, [and] that were born and raised in America"[27] —Westerns for their times were, according to Chuck Connors of *The Rifleman* and *Branded*, "the American fairy tale."[28]

As such the timely message of the genre was welcomed. Viewers of television Westerns saw a nation of immigrants in the making. Here was their country in its formative years. Certainly, there were bad men inside the burgeoning new Eden, but they were being inexorably purged—routed out by good people and their emulable leaders—who lived unpretentiously by the word of their law and their God. In the Western motif, there was no compromising with outlawry.

Tying it all together was the immigrant's dream of new opportunity, a world in which to start again. Every Western settlement was the product of dreamers. Among the ranchers, homesteaders, bar girls, sheriffs, and other types who populated the video genre, there were few who had abandoned their illusions about a better tomorrow. This spirit was aptly summarized in the opening to "The Brothers of the Knife," an episode of *Wichita Town* telecast February 10, 1960.

> Somewhere along the line someone nailed two boards to a dream and called it Wichita. But when you suck in a lungful of that Kansas heat, or feel the whip-burn of the winter wind, you wonder why people ever come here. Like as not, it's often to get away from somethin' worse. And there's plenty worse. Here in Wichita the dream's still nailed to that board—the heat cools—and the wind dies.

It was reassuring to see the shooting of a vicious gunslinger or the jailing of an anarchistic malcontent. It made the world a safer place. In their allegiance to law and order, these programs defended the American system against destructive divisiveness. Their heroes were mythic outriders of freedom, defeating the enemies of democratic civility and ensuring for law-abiding individuals the right to pursue happiness.

These Westerns were samplers of Americana, not because Theodore Roosevelt appeared in an episode of *Law of the Plainsman* ("The Dude" aired December 3, 1959) or Mark Twain met the Cartwrights of *Bonanza* ("Enter Mark Twain" aired October 10, 1959), or Phineas T. Barnum hired Jason McCord on *Branded* ("The Greatest Coward on Earth" aired November 21, 1965), but because in general they were compelling nationalistic homages that communicated an understandable and desirable interpretation of American social liberties and moral truths.

TV Westerns spoke directly to the innocence of American thought. They flattered their audiences by honoring the idealistic and lionizing self-sacrifice in the national past. Terming the hero of the genre a "six-gun Galahad," *Time* magazine in 1959 argued that the Western was "the great American morality play," a mythic scenario "in which Good and Evil, Spirit and Nature, Christian and Pagan fight to the finish on the vast stage of the unbroken plain." At its base, according to the *Time* interpretation, the Western proclaimed as its transcendent theme, the notion of human freedom.

> In the freedom of the great plains the story of the West had its beginnings; in the freedom of the heart it seems to seek its end. In its finest expression, it is an allegory of freedom, a memory and a vision of the deepest meaning of America.[29]

Yet, in a nation locked in a global contest with evil Communism, fearful of its future, and relatively inexperienced in great power international rivalries, matters such as human freedom were perforce politically partisan. Freedom was "ours"; slavery was "theirs." We were like those cowboy champions of liberty; they were like the outlaws who would enchain the body and crush the human spirit.

Writing in the politically conservative *National Review*, William F. Rickenbacker at the time of the Cuban missile crisis touched upon the patriotic quality of the genre. As the two superpowers stood at the brink of global nuclear war, Rickenbacker found strength in Westerns, for they

> speak a language very close to the heart of the American Dream: the dream of righteousness, the flowering of personal virtue and the power that flows therefrom, the selfless battle against Evil, a simple moral code, a sense of community, the respect for the poor, for the downtrodden, for the tempest tossed.[30]

Such nationalistic interpretation of the Western, however, was as selective as it was simple. For a genre that stressed transcendent notions of human freedom, the fate of the Indians in such programs was contradictory. In reality, the Americanization of the West entailed the conquest and subjugation of those living for centuries in the "wilderness," the Native Americans. The Indians actually lost their freedom in the westward push of the white settlers from the East, fulfilling a self-conceived Manifest Destiny.

As for the American Dream, during the nineteenth and twentieth centuries it often had a nightmarish history of exclusion, exploitation, and distortion. This was especially true as it applied to racial and religious minorities, industrial laborers, and women. Few Westerns communicated this reality through their stories.

Furthermore, despite the message in many Westerns, the United States did not possess the only blueprint for human happiness. Throughout the world there were other viable patterns of social freedom, economic and governmental success, and civil harmony. Not everyone prized individual initiative within a competitive, *laissez-faire* economic system—most of the world relied on various cooperative or communal arrangements. Not everyone sought personal fulfillment within capitalistic free enterprise—achievement and happiness were still possible within societies marked by agricultural self-sufficiency, state-planned economies, and even the varieties of socialism. Yet, the Western implied that the socioeconomic forms established in the United States by heroic pioneers and cowboys were universal standards—the best mankind could devise, the most mankind could want.

In doing so, the genre had difficulty addressing historical shortcomings. The true history of the westward expansion is the story of U.S. imperialism—of political intrigue, territorial conquest, nations defeated and dominated, and socioeconomic hegemony obtained and sometimes maintained through physical prowess. But the Western thrived on innocence: honest motives for its champions, respectful admiration by its viewers. Flattering and self-congratulatory, the Western confessed nothing.

At the height of their popularity, video Westerns provided a useful explanation of individual and national responsibilities in the world. Although their stories were fictional, audiences could accept as essentially accurate the portrait they painted of American civilization chronically threatened by lawlessness. As explained in 1961 by Clint Eastwood, who portrayed Rowdy Yates in *Rawhide*, "I like to think that *Rawhide* is honest. We're doing stories as they happened. Generally speaking, we're doing the kind of things that guys really did on the cattle drives."[31]

Such programs spiritually linked audiences to the spread of U.S. domination over the frontier. Each drama suggested that modern Americans were heirs to a legacy of noble hopes and sacrifices from patriotic predecessors. The editor of a Western magazine touched upon this spiritual kinship when he wrote in 1958:

Though we are a peaceful people at heart, we let no one push us around, and find a warm kinship in reading of the Westerners who wouldn't be pushed either, and who so colorfully retaliated with six guns, fists or lariat.[32]

Important to this nationalistic lesson was the image of the wilderness inherent in the Western. In reality the various Indian tribes populating the central and western portions of North America were flourishing civilizations complete with sophisticated political, economic, social, and religiomoralistic systems. There were also other nation-states with historic claims to parcels of that frontier. But such matters were seldom treated seriously by television Westerns.

The video West was all American, and that meant Caucasian, most likely Anglo-Saxon, and usually Protestant. When they were depicted, Native Americans were generally portrayed in one of three ways: noble anachronisms in the way of the white expansion; hostile savages harassing the innocent and disrupting the march of history; or, less frequently, assimilated and often fighting in the name of white social dominance.

Even when they were portrayed in this latter guise, Native Americans were expected to deal rationally with the abuse they received from whites. Typically, in "The Indian," an episode of *The Rifleman* aired February 17, 1959—which introduced Michael Ansara as Sam Buckhart, a Harvard-educated U.S. Marshal and the central character of his own series, *Law of the Plainsman*, that fall—a lawman faced racial derision and threats on his life from otherwise law-abiding settlers, this because he was an Apache Indian and he was arresting a white man for murder.

If Buckhart was ridiculed by most of the whites he encountered, as a "tamed one" he demonstrated classic distaste for those Indians who operated outside the laws of their conquerors. He made this clear in "The Raid," a second episode of *The Rifleman*—telecast June 9, 1959—in which he appeared. Here, while following Apaches who had kidnapped Lucas McCain's son, Buckhart explained to his white friend the nature of those he was tracking:

You know the Cherokee, but I know the Apache. I know what must be done. I know that if their senses warn them that something is wrong, you've gotta stop breathing, stop living, stop being for the moment. And you have to think of happy things. And don't sweat because they can smell it and it'll kill you. You don't attack by day, but lie quiet,

wait, and crawl. Crawl so they will not see you. Crawl so they will not
hear you. You must kill them in the darkness, Lucas. Even the Apache
must sleep. That's when you must take them, Lucas, when they sleep.
Toomey is right, the Apache does not give back prisoners.

Such depictions prompted Indian rights groups to protest vigor-
ously against the perpetuation of outdated racial stereotypes. In 1960
the Organization of Oklahoma Indian Tribes and the Association on
American Indian Affairs (AAIA) criticized network television for its
distortions of Native Americans. While the AAIA approved of Native
American representations in *Law of the Plainsman, The Lone Ranger,
Gunsmoke,* and *Have Gun—Will Travel,* it attacked series such as
Wagon Train where "Indians are shown as drunken, cowardly outlaws" and "usually attacking wagon trains." The organization assailed
the imagery on *Laramie* where Indians were depicted "holding white
girls captive, in addition to other brutal action." And it complained
that on *The Overland Trail* Native Americans were shown as "un-
believably stupid savages, believing in the most ridiculous witch-
craft."[33]

In response to this outcry, the Oklahoma state legislature in 1960
passed a resolution condemning network television for its treatment
of Indians.

> There is no excuse for TV producers to ignore the harm that may be
> done the children of America by repetitious distortion of historical facts
> pertaining to the way of life of any race or creed, including the American
> Indian. Many TV programs show Indians as bloodthirsty marauders and
> murderers.[34]

At a time when civil rights sensibilities fostered racial pride and
encouraged all minorities to protest their representation in American
popular culture, traditional stereotypes were subject to criticism by
activists. As late as 1971, for example, the Boston Indian Council
protested syndicated reruns of *Daniel Boone* as being little more than
white racist indoctrination especially detrimental to Native American
children. Through local courts of law, a special Indian Committee was
allowed to preview the *Daniel Boone* films and eventually delete 37
of the 165 episodes because they depicted "Indians scalping settlers,
burning, dragging women, being called savage, red devils, painted
devils, red monsters."[35]

Among other racial populations traditionally abused in the Western were the Asians. In reality they played an integral role in building
the West. Asian labor was especially important to the construction of

the railroad, which tied the Far West socially and commercially with the rest of the nation. In the video West, however, Asians were relegated to traditional stereotypes as cooks and experts in laundry. When a program like *The Wild, Wild West* was set in San Francisco, Chinese would appear as shadowy criminal types preoccupied with Tong wars and criminal plots against white men. The characters Hey Boy and Hey Girl on *Have Gun—Will Travel* and Hop Sing on *Bonanza* preserved the image of the comic, childlike Chinese servant happy to serve tolerant Caucasians. In only a few instances—such as "The Queue," a *Gunsmoke* episode aired December 3, 1955—did the genre display the Chinese as culturally proud and dignified and victimized by frontier bigotry.

Not until 1972 and the appearance of Kwai Chang Caine, the central character of *Kung Fu*, did the TV Western offer an Asian character who was more recognizably human. Nonetheless, even this character had his familiar limitations: he was depicted with "inscrutable" Oriental mystery, he was prone to Charlie Chan-styled aphorisms, he was half Caucasian, and he was portrayed by a non-Asian actor. Furthermore, although the Chinese-American actor Bruce Lee—who appeared in 1966-67 as Kato in *The Green Hornet* and became in the 1970s an internationally successful star of karate movies made in Hong Kong—was a consultant to those developing *Kung Fu*, he was rejected for the leading role, reportedly because the producers felt a Chinese actor could not be accepted as a hero by the American television audience.[36]

Other racial groups, particularly Afro-Americans, were scarce in the video Western. In reality, according to Philip Durham, "the negro cowboy, after the Civil War, moved out across the plains to play a significant role in the development of the cattle industry and became a part of the spirit of the West—a spirit which demanded a conscience, but cared little for color."[37] As historian William Loren Katz has explained it, in the authentic West black cowboys, gamblers, lawmen, and outlaws were an obvious part of the landscape. These characters included men and women. Blacks also were plentiful on the frontier for by 1890 there were half a million black men, women, and children living just in Texas and Oklahoma.[38]

Yet on television, the black experience was practically nonexistent. Except for a minor supporting role or infrequent guest appearance by blacks on a few series such as *Rawhide, Gunsmoke, Bonanza,* and *Johnny Ringo* there was little room on American video for anyone except Caucasians. The only series with an Afro-American in the leading role was *The Outcasts* on ABC during 1968-69. In this short-lived, controversial program black Otis Young and white Don Murray appeared as bounty hunters who were reluctant partners. Symbolizing the necessity for blacks and whites to work together in contemporary America, Young and Murray battled frontier hardships while struggling to keep their uneasy alliance alive.[39]

If there was racial prejudice in the television Western, there also was consistent historical distortion. The actual history of the West was not one of unprotested U.S. expansion. In the nineteenth century the North American frontier was a hotly contested political vacuum. As well as the Indian nations that warred on the white expansionists, several foreign governments maneuvered to arrest the westward thrust of the United States. These included Great Britain, France, Canada, Mexico, and Spain.

In the TV West, however, these antagonistic nationalities were inconsequential. The heroes of the video dramas fought to defeat generic injustice, not to revive long-forgotten international boundary disputes. Television entertainment did not try to give history lessons to the uninformed.

On TV the wilds of North America were projected as a providential gift to the United States. There was never a doubt the continental expanse would be Americanized. In fact, the entire area appeared as little more than a vacant wasteland eager to accept political and military control from Washington and breathlessly awaiting integration into the republic.

Such innocent imagery was crucial to the TV Western of the 1950s and 1960s. Indeed, such interpretation was a chronic function of a genre that, according to the French film critic Andre Bazin, should not be judged "by the yardstick of archeology."[40] The Western proclaimed its message in a streamlined historic past that was modified by the present according to cultural specifications that were reassuring and uncompromising. The TV Western fit the temper of the times. It helped to explain the problems of the world.

While no such series had an overt, flag-waving patriot as its central character, the symbolism within the genre was relevant to a nation locked in international competition. A triumph in the video Old West may have been popular cultural escapism, but it was also metaphorical victory for American goodness in the modern West. Pride in the achievements of Major Seth Adams of *Wagon Train* or the Barkley family of *The Big Valley* translated into pride in the contemporary

United States, the nation created ultimately by their vision and courage. Such spiritual connection flowed inevitably from the genre, for as Thomas Schatz has written, "As America's foundation ritual, the Western projects a formalized vision of the nation's infinite possibilities and limitless vistas."[4] [1]

To accept such a preponderant number of Westerns on prime-time television in the 1950s and 1960s, viewers had to approve of the community being forged or defended in each episode. In this manner, then, the Western heroes on TV were symbolic Cold Warriors. They showed how to win against treachery; they demonstrated that it was not necessary to coexist with evil.

In their characters and achievements Wyatt Earp, Lucas McCain, Cheyenne Bodie, and their video peers amalgamated historical precedent and modern dedication, all in justification of American prerogatives. They may have been fantasy heroes, but they were winners. It was an inescapable moral lesson. In a time of challenge, the television Western was relevant drama.

DEMISE OF THE GENRE

For the Western to have continued to inundate network TV, or even to have survived as viable video diversion, the mass audience would have had to maintain its taste for the mentality fundamental to this entertainment format. This did not happen.

As well as raising primal doubts regarding the Western as legal, moral, and political drama, momentous events of the 1960s and after have altered popular understanding of the attitudes and values that made the genre so widely accepted. The exposure of overwhelming and chronic civil rights injustices in the United States debased the image of freedom and human dignity so lavishly reinforced in the Western. A divisive war and defeat in Southeast Asia revealed the inglorious truth about militarism and death—themes that Hollywood frontier dramas usually romanticized. Although there had been a chronic critique of violence on television, the nightly slaughter of the Vietnam War on TV seemed to saturate American culture with violence, thereby rendering excessive, even obscene, the mayhem integral to the Western.

Other factors eroded the spirit of the genre. Scandals surrounding the White House undermined the political solemnity inherent in the Western. The women's movement—which in the 1970s precipitated a social, economic, political, and historical reappraisal of the role of American women—aggressively confronted the preponderant machismo of the genre. The ineffectiveness of the U.S. response in the global struggle against civil war and terrorism in the Third World also mitigated against the Western's myth of the invincibility of the United States.

The undermining of self-perceptions fundamental to a century of American sociopolitical life has meant the death of the principal genre of romanticized, quasihistorical entertainment in the United States. Where no outlaw's bullet could fell the Cartwrights of *Bonanza*, mass cynicism caused them to vanish from NBC in January 1973. Although Matt Dillon and *Gunsmoke* survived on CBS for two decades, they died unceremoniously in 1975, anachronisms in an era of social reevaluation.

Actually, as early as the fall of 1967 the fate of the TV Western was foreshadowed in the case of *Custer*, an ABC series based freely on the frontier exploits of Lt. Col. George Armstrong Custer. Whatever expectations the network or its producer, 20th Century-Fox Television, had for the series, *Custer* was out of date from its inception.

Even before its first telecast, Native American organizations assailed the program as detrimental to Indians. The protest began with Sioux Indians in South Dakota. More than 24,000 Chippewa Indians in Minnesota then criticized it, alleging, in the words of a spokesman, "The *Custer* series will stir up old animosities and revive Indian and cowboy fallacies we have been trying to live down."[42] Following the premier show, the National Congress of the American Indian demanded equal time to reply to the misrepresentations it detected.[43]

The series itself offered an outdated image of the Old West. The depiction of savage Indians slaughtering white men was offensive to civil rights groups, and especially to Native Americans. The brutality of the stories—from knife fights to scalpings to old-fashioned cavalry charges—violated the sensibilities of many critical of TV violence. A bear-hunting expedition offended those sensitive to ecological issues. The masculine emphases of the series inhibited female interest.

The distortions of frontier history in *Custer* were also pronounced. Those seeking historical reconstruction or even accuracy were discouraged.[44] The stress on military glory in *Custer* ran counter to a growing public debate by 1967 over the military role of the United States in the Vietnam War. To this were added scripts in which, for example, Custer insensitively could tell his troops, "As professional soldiers, we'd best leave the question of morality to those whose job it is. Our job is to fight." The series was canceled after half a season.

Larry White, vice president for programming at NBC, touched upon the predicament of the TV Western by the early 1970s when he remarked that "the younger audience seems not to have an appetite for westerns." Speaking in 1972 White added, "Younger people today are 25 years farther removed from the Old West" and are not really interested in what they consider an oversimplification of history. Moreover, he concluded, the black-and-white hues of the Western formula simply appeal no longer to the younger generation.[45]

Indeed, by the early 1970s youthful interest in the Western had diminished significantly. A study of children in the first, sixth, and tenth grades found that as the favorite type of television program, the

Table 10   Children's Favorite Programs, Early 1970s (by grade levels, percent, ranking)

Program Type	First Grade		Sixth Grade		Tenth Grade	
	Percent	Rank	Percent	Rank	Percent	Rank
Youth-oriented adventure	10	4	14	3	20	1
Situation comedy	22	3	17	2	9	3*
Family situation comedy	25	1	23	1	9	3*
Police/detective	3	6*	5	6*	6	5*
Cartoon/kiddie	24	2	5	6*	6	5*
Music/variety/talk	3	6*	5	6*	13	2*
Serial dramas	—	—	3	8*	9	3*
Dramatic	2	7*	6	5	13	2*
News	—	—	1	10	1	7
Education/culture	4	5	3	8*	2	6*
Western	3	6*	8	4	7	4
Game shows	2	7*	4	7*	2	6*
Sports	—	—	2	9	2	6*
Movies	2	7*	4	7*	6	5*

*Indicates a tie.

Source: As adapted from George A. Comstock, Steve Chaffee et al., *Television and Human Behavior* (New York: Columbia University Press, 1975), p. 184; and J. Lyle and H. R. Hoffman, "Children's Use of Television and Other Media," in *Television and Social Behavior*, Vol. IV: *Television in Day-to-Day Life: Patterns of Use*, ed. E. A. Rubinstein, George A. Comstock, and J. P. Murray (Washington, D.C.: U.S. Government Printing Office, 1972), pp. 129-256.

Western rated far behind situation comedy, police/detective shows, drama, and the like. According to Table 10, in the three school groups the Western was no longer popular.

Ironically, there had been those who felt the Western would never die as a television form. Usually a prescient observer of American popular cultural trends, Les Brown in *Variety* declared as late as December 1965 that the "Western has become a staple of television and probably will always remain one."[46] Earlier Nat Holt, producer of *Tales of Wells Fargo*, saw only a bright future for the genre. In 1959 he pointed out that since the beginning of the film industry one-quarter of all movies had been Westerns. Now on TV, he maintained, "people want Westerns, and you can't take away something they want."[47] Both Brown and Holt were shortsighted. By the mid-1970s the Western was virtually gone from network television. Except for a few old series crawling toward cancellation, audiences apparently no longer wanted such programming.

Nevertheless, there were many attempts after 1970 to revive the genre. New series with novel emphases ranged from exploitation of contemporary martial arts techniques (*Kung Fu*) to new sensitivities toward the experiences of women in the Old West (*Sara*) and Native Americans in the modern West (*Cade's County*). There were short-term miniseries (*The Sacketts*), longer-running historical epics (*Centennial*), and one miniseries became a regular series (*The Chisolms*).

Some of the biggest names in the popular arts were enlisted, including the Walt Disney studio (*Zorro and Son* and *Wildside*) and author Louis L'Amour (*The Sacketts*). Disney executives even joined forces with the most successful writer of Western novels when they produced *Louis L'Amour's The Cherokee Trail*, an unsuccessful pilot shown on CBS in November 1981.

Popular motion pictures about frontier life inspired several TV series. Thus the charmingly irreverent *Butch Cassidy and the Sundance Kid* begat the self-consciously irreverent *Alias Smith and Jones. The Cowboys*, a feature film starring John Wayne, led less imaginatively to *The Cowboys*, a television Western featuring Jim Davis. Two motion pictures from Sweden, *The Emigrants* and *The New Land*—features that told of the Swedish settlers in frontier Minnesota in the mid-nineteenth century—inspired the TV series, *The New Land*.

Younger viewers, so sizable a segment of the television audience, were approached directly in *Young Dan'l Boone, The Young Pioneers,* and *The Cowboys*. The first offered the famous Kentucky backwoodsman while still in his midtwenties. *The Young Pioneers* featured the tribulations of teenage newlyweds in the Dakota wilderness in the 1870s. *The Cowboys* told of seven children—the oldest being 15 years of age—running a cattle ranch for a sympathetic widow.

For those who preferred their Western heroes grizzled and well-experienced, *Hec Ramsey* was a scruffy oldtimer confronting up-to-date methods of criminal detection as deputy sheriff in the pioneering town of New Prospect, Oklahoma. *Dirty Sally* concerned a cantankerous, liquor-drinking old woman moving toward the gold fields of California accompanied by a young ex-gunfighter and a mule named Worthless.

One of the most powerful productions in this search for the acceptable Western was *The Quest*. In its desire to be relevant, this series in the fall of 1976 offered an alluring mix of violence, youthful initiative, sympathy for racial minorities, and antimilitarism. Set in the 1870s, the program concerned two orphaned and separated brothers—one raised on the plains by Cheyenne Indians, the other a medical school graduate who grew up in San Francisco—who were now reunited in quest of their sister, herself taken years earlier by Indians.

In the 11 episodes that aired on CBS, *The Quest* employed violence to picture the West as a brutal, sinister, and unhappy domain. In the premier program the brothers helped the U.S. Cavalry "rescue" a young white woman who had lived for years with Indians. During their bloody raid on her village, the American troops were shown callously shooting women and children fleeing the attackers. Removed to the white man's civilization, the young woman was raped by a sadistic soldier, then rejected by bigoted townspeople who disliked her past association with Indians.

Another offering of *The Quest* concerned the importation of Chinese strike-breakers whose appearance incited antibusiness and anti-Asian prejudices in the citizens of a wilderness settlement. Still another program dealt with a lusty bordello operator whose civic-mindedness matched her acumen for peddling women's sexual favors.

Stark meanness permeated *The Quest*. Whether it was a crazed Texas Ranger who preferred to hang newly captured suspects on the spot, or the unsympathetic words of an animalistic buffalo hunter who encased one of the brothers in a shrinking leather hide—"He'll stay till he's squoze to jelly . . . till his head busts like a squashed melon"—this was a brutish series that attempted to interpret American frontier history in terms of the conflicting political passions that followed U.S. humiliation in the Vietnam War. Critic Robert MacKenzie summarized the intention and vulnerability of *The Quest* when he wrote:

"Every generation remakes the Western in its own image; here it is the setting for the mean streets and starved spirits of modern urban life."[48]

Much imagination was expended in the attempt to revive the anachronistic genre. The predilection for fanciful disguises so popular in the 1960s on *The Wild Wild West*, appeared now in *The Barbary Coast*. There was a prime-time soap opera set on a modern Texas ranch (*The Yellow Rose*). To bring wit to Western drama James Garner, the popular leading man of the vintage *Maverick* program, remounted his horse to introduce one new series (*Young Maverick*) and to star in two others (*Nichols* and *Bret Maverick*).

To bring farce to the genre, there were cowboy situation comedies like *Zorro and Son, Best of the West,* and *Gun Shy*. Perhaps the most ambitious of these laughable Westerns, however, was *Dusty's Trail*, a syndicated series in 1973 that tried to resuscitate the genre by filling its cast with alumni of earlier sitcom hits such as *Gilligan's Island, Petticoat Junction,* and *F Troop*.

The expenditure of Hollywood imagination was not enough, however. As Table 11 indicates, whatever the stylization or gimmick, few Western series introduced since 1970 achieved even moderate success.

Producers invested millions of dollars seeking a formula with which to regenerate viewer interest in Westerns. The most elaborate project was *How the West Was Won*. Inspired by the epic Cinerama motion picture from 1963 of the same name, it first came to television in January 1976 as a telefeature called *The Macahans*. With its lush outdoor photography, sweeping sense of frontier history, energetic promotion, and veteran actor James Arness as its star, *How the West Was Won* appeared in February 1977 as a six-hour miniseries. It then appeared in the first half of 1978 as a weekly series.[49]

After reruns that summer, the program was dropped, only to reappear for four months in early 1979 with nine new installments budgeted at $1.2 million per two-hour episode. Except for its short run in 1978, however, *How the West Was Won* failed to garner audiences large enough to justify its continuance.

Not only were video Westerns unsuccessful, their failure rate after 1970 was devastating. The majority of these programs lasted a half-season or less. *Young Maverick* was aired eight times. *The New Land, Wildside,* and *Gun Shy* appeared only six times each. *The Oregon Trail* was seen on four occasions. Only three episodes each of *Young Dan'l Boone* and *The Young Pioneers* were telecast. In the years 1972-74,

Table 11 Western Series Introduced since 1970

Title	Years	Rating	Ranking	Total Ranked
Cade's County	1971-72	17.0	49*	78
Nichols	1971-72	13.2	64*	78
Alias Smith and Jones	1971-72	16.1	55	78
Alias Smith and Jones	1972-73	9.6	72*	75
Kung Fu	1972-73	19.2	32*	75
Kung Fu	1973-74	18.7	36	81
Dirty Sally	1974	17.8	43*	81
The Cowboys	1974	15.8	59*	81
Kung Fu	1974-75	9.9	82*	84
The New Land	1974	7.9	84	84
The Barbary Coast	1975-76	11.2	93	97
Sara	1976	13.4	79*	97
The Quest	1976-77	12.9	91*	101
The Young Pioneers	1977-78	13.5	93*	109
Young Dan'l Boone	1977-78	13.8	88*	109
The Oregon Trail	1977-78	14.3	82*	109
How the West Was Won	1978	21.4	17*	109
How the West Was Won	1978-79	18.0	46	112
Centennial	1978-79	19.5	33*	112
Young Maverick	1979-80	13.4	88	105
The Chisolms	1979-80	13.2	89*	105
Bret Maverick	1981-82	17.7	34	105
Best of the West	1981-82	13.9	71	105
Zorro and Son	1982-83	12.6	78	98
Gun Shy	1983	12.1	82*	98
The Yellow Rose	1983-84	10.1	90*	101
Wildside	1984-85	11.5	82	97

*Indicates a tie.

Source: Statistics come from the annual summary of Nielsen ratings as printed in *Variety*, May 24, 1972, p. 35; May 30, 1973, p. 30; May 8, 1974, p. 262; May 14, 1975, p. 132; April 28, 1976, p. 44; April 27, 1977, p. 50; May 3, 1978, p. 54; May 23, 1979, p. 52; June 4, 1980, p. 48; June 10, 1981, p. 36; May 12, 1982, pp. 452, 457; May 11, 1983, p. 56; April 25, 1984, pp. 76, 80; May 1, 1985, p. 468.

Hec Ramsey rotated with three other series as part of *The NBC Sunday Mystery Movie*; but only ten installments of this Western were telecast, while others in the rotation—*McMillan and Wife, Columbo,* and *McCloud*—lasted for five seasons.

While Westerns in recent decades have been poorly received as weekly television fare, they also have failed in those special projects that are called made-for-TV films and miniseries. In the 20 years between October 1964 and July 1984, there were 1,693 dramatic productions filmed expressly for network television, the vast majority being made-for-TV movies aired on showcases such as *The ABC Movie of the Week* and *NBC Wednesday Night at the Movies.*

Significantly, only 92 of these films—little more than 5.4 percent—were Westerns. These ranged from the 26.5 hours of the miniseries *Centennial,* to TV movies as diverse as the comedic *Evil Roy Slade* (February 18, 1972), the nostalgic *The Wild, Wild West Revisited* (May 9, 1979), the modern *Rodeo Girl* (September 17, 1980), and the youth-oriented *Peter Lundy and the Medicine Hat Stallion* (November 6, 1977)—as well as Don Siegel's direction of Henry Fonda in *Stranger on the Run* (October 31, 1969), the memorable if controversial Indian saga *The Mystic Warrior* (May 20-21, 1984), and the

Table 12   Made-for-TV Western Films and Miniseries, 1964-84

Year	Number/Total	Percent	Year	Number/Total	Percent
1964	0/2	0	1975	4/105	3.8
1965	0/0	0	1976	11/90	12.2
1966	2/4	50.0	1977	6/123	4.9
1967	3/10	30.0	1978	12/149	8.1
1968	1/14	7.1	1979	6/152	3.9
1969	2/30	6.7	1980	4/149	2.7
1970	5/44	11.3	1981	2/125	1.6
1971	6/83	7.2	1982	3/116	2.6
1972	6/83	7.2	1983	4/120	3.3
1973	2/107	1.9	1984	3/69	4.3
1974	7/118	5.9			

Source: Statistical information is drawn from Alvin H. Marill, *Movies Made for Television: The Telefeature and the Mini-Series 1964-1984* (New York: New York Zoetrope, 1985). Researchers using this source must be careful of the sloppy numbering of films cited in this book as some numbers have been omitted and other numbers have been cited twice.

more forgettable Indian tale *The Legend of Walks Far Woman* (May 30, 1982).

That the networks have been parsimonious in airing Western tele-features and miniseries is made obvious by the statistics in Table 12. Except for the years around the U.S. bicentennial observances, made-for-TV Westerns have been rare, a small part of the annual totals.

As well as scarce, made-for-TV Westerns have been ratings disasters. In its survey of hit movies on U.S. television from 1961 through 1985, *Variety* listed 506 telecasts that garnered at least a Nielsen rating of 24.0. While several theatrical Westerns have achieved high rankings—*Jeremiah Johnson* tied for number 13, *The Apple Dumpling Gang* tied for number 44, *Butch Cassidy and the Sundance Kid* tied at number 46, plus several cowboy dramas starring John Wayne and Clint Eastwood—only 11 made-for-TV Westerns (actually only 10 different films) appear in this listing, little more than 2 percent of the total.

The most successful Western telefeature was *Kenny Rogers As the Gambler*, a film that exploited Rogers's hit phonograph record, "The Gambler." It was the most popular made-for-TV film in the 1979-80 season; and it was tied at number 58 in the survey published in *Variety* (see Table 13). Interestingly, the next highest rated made-for-TV

Table 13 Hit Made-for-TV Western Films

Rank	Title	Rating/Share	Date of Telecast
59*	Kenny Rogers As the Gambler	31.3/50	4/8/80
89*	Kenny Rogers As the Gambler —The Adventure Continues (Part II)	29.6/45	11/29/83
92*	Kenny Rogers As the Gambler —The Adventure Continues (Part I)	29.5/42	11/28/83
92*	Mrs. Sundance	29.5/43	4/9/74
99*	Alias Smith and Jones	29.3/44	1/5/71
161*	Run, Simon, Run	27.5/43	12/1/70
179*	Hardcase	27.2/40	2/1/72
203*	The Over-the-Hill Gang	26.8/42	10/7/79
311*	The Young Pioneers	25.5/37	3/1/76
362*	The Daughters of Joshue Cabe	25.0/38	9/13/72
457*	The Bravos	24.2/38	1/9/72

*Indicates a tie.
Source: Variety, January 8, 1986, pp. 172, 179, 189.

Westerns were the two parts of a sequel miniseries, *Kenny Rogers As the Gambler—The Adventure Continues*, telecast more than three years after the original Rogers telefeature.

Not only do these figures suggest the consistent failure of the made-for-TV Western, they also demonstrate that the genre had been moribund for a long time. Seven of the ranked telecasts were from the late 1960s and early 1970s. In the past decade only the Rogers efforts attracted large audiences. Further, three were light-hearted Westerns (*The Over-the-Hill Gang, Mrs. Sundance,* and *Alias Smith and Jones*) which parodize the genre. The popularity of several can be understood in terms of attractiveness of their stars: Burt Reynolds in *Run, Simon, Run*; Buddy Ebsen in *The Daughters of Joshua Cabe*; plus the three telecasts featuring Kenny Rogers. When the record of made-for-TV Westerns is added to the performance of regular Western series since 1970, it seems obvious that Americans have abandoned the genre.

Clearly, the cultural synchronization—the matching of popular values with the themes and perspectives inherent in an entertainment form—needed for continued commercial and social acceptance has been lost. Western heroes, now out of joint with popular thought, have ridden into oblivion.

That the TV Western has perished is made all the more certain by the nature of television. Unlike media such as radio, musical recording, and literature, TV in the United States still courts an undifferentiated mass viewership. Where other commercial media serve a multiplicity of small demographic units, network video remains tightly competitive between three corporations seeking the same broad, diverse audience for their offerings.

For almost 30 years radio has cultivated *narrow*casting as an answer to the financial ruin guaranteed by continuing to seek the widest audience via *broad*casting. The recording industry today is not just Top-40 popular music. It is a variegated phenomenon offering commercial musical products for a diversity of tastes. From fancy bookstores to local magazine racks the narrowest literary interests are accommodated in American publishing.

Even so, programming on network television remains a mass medium in which a program survives only if it delivers acceptably high ratings. It is not enough that a series delivers a few million viewers; it must attract many millions of viewers. There are thousands of radio stations, records, and publishers, but there are only three outlets for hit TV programming: ABC, CBS, and NBC. While loyal readers continue to purchase the formulaic novels of Louis L'Amour, relative to a television audience they constitute a small following. While country-western music is a lucrative part of the music and radio industries, this related taste has not translated into sizable support for video Westerns.

The Western is dead in television because it is no longer relevant or tasteful. Economic and technological realities of the medium only assure that it will not be successful until it regains mass acceptability. Ironically, the generation that once made the Western the most prolific form of TV programming has lived to see a rare occurrence in American popular culture: the death of a genre.

NOTES

1. *Variety*, January 7, 1976, p. 101.

2. *Television Forecast* (Chicago), May 28, 1949, p. 2.

3. As cited in Nicholas Johnson, "Television and Violence—Perspectives and Proposals," *Television Quarterly* 8, no. 1 (Winter 1969):43. Earlier, Senator Dodd associated video with gambling, prostitution, rackets, and other social evils. He concluded: "We must determine if this gigantic new medium is not allowing similar human weaknesses to dictate its policies and drag it into the same category as the violent Roman spectacles of 2,000 years ago, which also had 'high ratings.'" See *Broadcasting*, June 12, 1961, p. 60.

4. See the article by Stockton Helffrich, NBC director of Continuity Acceptance, *Variety*, September 10, 1958, p. 38.

5. Newton N. Minow, "The Broadcasters Are Public Trustees," in *Radio and Television: Readings in the Mass Media*, ed. Allen Kirschner and Linda Kirschner (Indianapolis: Bobbs-Merrill, 1971), pp. 207-17. For a compelling retort to Minow's critique of commercial TV, see Roy B. Huggins, "The Bloodshot Eye: A Comment on the Crisis in American Television," *Television Quarterly* 1, no. 3 (August 1962):6-22.

6. William J. Millard, Jr., "A Research Study of *Wells Fargo*." February 11, 1957, p. 25. NBC Records, box 194, folder 29.

7. Cyril C. Wagner to Homer Heck (Foote, Cone & Belding), August 14, 1957. NBC Records, box 143, folder 17. Of related interest is the story concept for *Wagon Train* submitted in April 1957 by Richard Lewis, executive producer at Revue Productions for the forthcoming series. According to Lewis,

> the individual stories, while taking full advantage of all movement and action inherent in a Western will nevertheless be chosen primarily for their dramatic values and appeal to an adult audience, avoiding the tired formulae of the typical 'horseopera.' While these stories were primarily chosen for their emotional conflicts and general adult appeal, they also provide ample opportunity for two fisted action and violent climaxes.

Richard Lewis, "*Wagon Train* Story Concept," April 1957. NBC Records, box 143, folder 17.

8. The following discussion and direct quotations are drawn from the letter from David Levy to Robert W. Sarnoff, July 13, 1961. NBC Records.

9. On Newton Minow's speech and its place in the manipulation of commercial television by the Kennedy administration, see Mary Ann Rutkowski Watson, "Commercial Television and the New Frontier: Resistance and Appeasement," Ph.D. diss., University of Michigan, 1983.

10. *Variety*, October 27, 1971, p. 42.

11. Unpublished interview with Michael Marsden, March 1985, as cited in "The Making of *Gunsmoke*: The Writers," paper delivered at the 16th Annual Meeting of the Popular Culture Association, Atlanta, April 5, 1986. For John Mantley's views on the "communion" between *Gunsmoke* characters, see Horace Newcomb and Robert S. Alley, *The Producer's Medium: Conversations with Creators of American TV* (New York: Oxford University Press, 1983), p. 103.

For a complete log of *Gunsmoke* productions, including plot synopses, names of programs, directors, writers, as well as play dates, see Kristine Fredericksson, "*Gunsmoke*: Twenty-Year Videography," *Journal of Popular Film and Television*, XII:1 (Spring 1984), pp. 16-33; XII:2 (Summer 1984), pp. 73-86; XII:3 (Fall 1984), pp. 127-43; XII:4 (Winter 1984/85), pp. 171-86.

12. Dwight Whitney, "What's *Gunsmoke*'s Secret?," *TV Guide*, August 22, 1970, p. 25.

13. *Variety*, March 5, 1969, pp. 1, 86.

14. *Variety*, November 14, 1984, p. 41.

15. *Variety*, June 2, 1971, p. 27. See also Rose K. Goldsen, *The Show and Tell Machine. How Television Works and Works You Over* (New York: Dial Press, 1977), pp. 206-22.

16. Newcomb and Alley, *The Producer's Medium*, p. 103. Compare the more materialistic interpretation of the TV Western in Hal Himmelstein, *Television Myth and the American Mind* (New York: Praeger Publishers, 1984), pp. 170-75.

17. Jim Morse, "In Defense of Westerns and Private Eyes," *TV Radio Mirror*, May 1961, p. 70.

18. Julian Smith, *Looking Away. Hollywood and Vietnam* (New York: Charles Scribner's Sons, 1975), pp. 27-30.

19. Peter Homans, "The Western. The Legend and the Cardboard Hero," *Look*, March 13, 1962, p. 89. Also see the article by Homans, "Puritanism Revisited: An Analysis of the Contemporary Screen-Image Western," *Studies in Public Communication*, Summer 1961, pp. 73-84.

20. Martin Nussbaum, "Sociological Symbolism of the 'Adult' Western," *Social Forces*, October 1960, p. 27-28.

21. Alexander Miller, "The Western—A Theological Note," *The Christian Century*, November 27, 1957, p. 1410.

22. Herbert L. Jacobson, "Cowboy, Pioneer and American Soldier," *Sight and Sound*, April-June 1953, p. 190.

23. Leif Furhammar and Folke Isaksson, *Politics and Film* (New York: Praeger, 1968 and 1971), p. 59.

24. Loren Baritz, *Backfire: A History of How American Culture Led Us into Vietnam and Made Us Fight the Way We Did* (New York: Morrow, 1985), pp. 51-52.

25. David Shea Teeple, "TV Westerns Tell a Story," *The American Mercury*, April 1958, pp. 116-17.

26. For a broader discussion of television programming, the Western included, as an anti-Communist propagandizing force contributing to the national mentality that accepted and approved the Vietnam War, see J. Fred MacDonald, *Television and the Red Menace: The Video Road to Vietnam* (New York: Praeger, 1985).

27. James Horwitz, *They Went Thataway* (New York: Ballantine Books, 1978), p. 142.

28. *TV Guide*, January 23, 1965, p. 8.

29. *Time*, March 30, 1959, p. 60.

30. William F. Rickenbacker, "60,000,000 Westerners Can't Be Wrong," *National Review*, October 23, 1962, pp. 322-25.

31. Morse, "In Defense of Westerns and Private Eyes," p. 71.

32. Editor of *Top Western* magazine, as cited in John P. Sisk, "The Western Hero," *Commonweal,* July 12, 1957, p. 367.

33. New York *Times,* June 26, 1960. United States Commission on Civil Rights, *Window Dressing on the Set: Women and Minorities in Television* (Washington, D.C.: U.S. Government Printing Office, 1977), p. 6. For an early discussion of shortcomings in the video depiction of Native Americans, see *TV Guide,* April 19, 1958, pp. 13-15.

34. U.S. Commission on Civil Rights, *Window Dressing on the Set,* p. 6.

35. George W. Woolery, *Children's Television: The First Thirty-Five Years, 1946-1981. Part II: Live, Film, and Tape Series.* (Metuchen, N.J.: Scarecrow Press, 1985), p. 138.

36. Kareem Abdul-Jabbar and Peter Knobler, *Giant Steps: The Autobiography of Kareem Abdul-Jabbar* (New York: Bantam, 1983), pp. 188-89; as cited in Clint C. Wilson II and Felix Gutierrez, *Minorities and Media: Diversity and the End of Mass Communication* (Beverly Hills, Calif.: Sage Publications, 1985), pp. 101-02.

37. Philip Durham, "The Negro Cowboy," in *The American Experience: Approaches to the Study of the United States,* ed. Hennig Cohen (Boston: Houghton Mifflin, 1968), pp. 259-60. This article appeared originally *The American Quarterly,* Summer 1964. See also Durham's book, *The Negro Cowboys* (New York: Dodd, Mead, 1965).

38. William Loren Katz, *The Black West* (New York: Anchor Books, 1973), pp. 143ff.

39. On the matter of Afro-Americans in television Westerns, see J. Fred MacDonald, *Blacks and White TV: Afro-Americans in Television since 1948* (Chicago: Nelson-Hall, 1983), pp. 123-27.

40. Andre Bazin, *What Is Cinema?,* vol. II (Berkeley: University of California Press, 1971), p. 143.

41. Thomas Schatz, *Hollywood Genres: Formulas, Filmmaking, and the Studio System.* (Philadelphia: Temple University Press, 1981), p. 47.

42. *Variety,* September 13, 1967, p. 34; August 30, 1967, p. 32.

43. Ralph E. Friar and Natasha A. Friar, *The Only Good Indian . . . The Hollywood Gospel.* (New York: Drama Book Specialists, 1972), pp. 274-76.

44. P. M. Clepper, "Some Advice to the Producers of *Custer,*" *TV Guide,* September 23, 1967, pp. 32-34.

45. *Variety,* June 21, 1972, p. 31. Although he felt that "if there's a hell of a good western with very good stories and interesting actors, that show will succeed," by the late 1970s producer John Mantley still contended that "People are too sophisticated today to accept the old-fashioned western." Newcomb and Alley, *The Producer's Medium,* p. 120.

46. *Variety,* December 1, 1965, p. 28.

47. *Variety,* November 19, 1958, p. 31. For a cautious, if not really skeptical, contemporary assessment of the staying power of the Western, see Herman Land, "After the Western—What?," *Television Magazine,* July 1958, pp. 55-57.

48. Robert MacKenzie, "Review: *The Quest,*" *TV Guide,* October 30, 1976, p. 34.

49. Producer John Mantley blamed ABC for compelling him to restructure his series to fit network one-hour and two-hour time segments so that "America never saw one single show the way it was conceived, written, directed, and produced! Not one!!" Newcomb and Alley, *The Producer's Medium*, p. 116.

Epilogue

While they were popular, Westerns on television offered a social philosophy. Within their stylized traditions a viewer could find self-definition, values through which to comprehend his or her place in the world. Here, too, in its archetypes, symbols, and actions were metaphors justifying American policies in postwar politics. On a mass scale the TV Western provided a spiritual bonding between the heroic accomplishments of the old frontier and the individual and national obligations now confronting the new frontier.

Even at the time the video Western was perceived in monumental terms. It was *the* genre of the first two decades of television programming. As actor Barry Sullivan of *The Tall Man* declared confidently in 1961, "if Shakespeare were alive today, he'd be writing westerns."[1] Today, however, such presumption seems strikingly unrealistic. In fact, were Shakespeare writing Westerns in the last quarter of the twentieth century, he would be greatly out of joint with the times.

The failure of Western drama on network TV suggests an evolution within American popular thought. The death of the video Wild West meant a discrediting of the "cowboy mentality": that chronic tendency in American culture to approach sociopolitical life in terms of a rural democracy filled with black-and-white simplicity—where problems are basically uncomplicated and easily resolvable; where direct action, often violent and destructive, quickly brings justice and restores social stability; where entertainment based upon distorted history places all ethnic and racial groups, all generations, and both sexes in uncritical communion with venerated pioneering Caucasian fore*fathers*; and where horse-mounted, gun-toting heroes *cum* moral agents reassuringly return each week with a fresh child- or adult-oriented tale communicating notions of invincibility and rectitude.

The inability of the genre to survive represents, on the one hand, the failure of television writers and producers to discover the modifications—the new themes, language, and perspectives—necessary to rescue it from irrelevance. Into the second half of the 1980s, with aspects of its meaning co-opted by space adventures, urban police dramas, seductive prime-time soap operas, and even situation comedies, there seemingly exists no reason to expect its resurrection. Born a literary genre in the nineteenth century, the Western as TV fare faces the possibility of extinction by the twenty-first century.

Even a trend toward political conservatism in the 1980s has failed to enliven the genre. Despite the impressive popularity of an ideologically conservative leader like Ronald Reagan, the Western on television has continued in its decline. The jingoism in successful theatrical features such as *Red Dawn, Rocky IV, Invasion U.S.A.,* and two *Rambo* films has meant little to the revival of the Western. Even cowboy films like *Rustler's Rhapsody, Silverado,* and Clint Eastwood's *Pale Rider* have been few and, despite the drawing power of a leading man like Eastwood, less than successful at the box office.

As with the 1985-86 television year, there were no Western series scheduled for the 1986-87 season. *TV Guide* reported that NBC and CBS had pilot films in development and that CBS ordered six episodes of a series in which "several desperadoes of the 1890s are suddenly transported to the present." As for ABC, "having endured the failure of *Wildside* last year, [it] has no Westerns in development."[2]

Perhaps the most ironic comment on the disintegration of the genre appeared in an advertisement promising for the fall of 1987 a syndicated new cartoon series, *Saber Rider and the Star Sheriffs,* a hybrid of futuristic science fiction and the Western. "An out-of-this-world futuristic fantasy with a Western twist," proclaimed the full-page announcement in *Variety* in mid-1986. "Combine the legendary honor, virtue and individualism of the Wild West with vibrant extra-terrestrial adventure," it continued. This evisceration of the Western would be accomplished through an animated cast that included Saber Rider, "handsome leader on his magnificient Steed pitted against the galaxy's slickest rustlers, a hero waging the battle for liberty and justice"—and Colt, "bold teenage cowboy pilot of the flashy Bronco-buster, he's the galaxy's sharpest shooter"—and April, "heartthrob of the whole galaxy and a cool and steely defender in the face of danger."[3]

The demise of the TV Western signifies a new level of national awareness. Despite nostalgic trends in contemporary political and religious leadership, life for the majority of Americans remains an urban ambiguity—a world of compromises with city life and modern technology in which workable answers are not readily forthcoming. While escapist fantasies set in an expansionist, pre-industrial United States might reappear occasionally in American popular culture, urban routine has become a prepossessing fact of life. The image of a messenger of Truth dressed in spurs, wearing a wide-brimmed hat, and carrying a pair of revolvers on his hips seems rediculously unbelievable, if not popularly discredited.

Today the genre has been relegated to reruns of old series on local stations. Interestingly, the principal consumer of syndicated Westerns from the 1950s and 1960s is the lowly-rated cable service of the Christian Broadcasting Network. For this politically-conservative, religiously fundamentalist operation, early evenings and weekends are deeply committed to vintage cowboy shows. Whether the motives of CBN are political, religious, or economic, through the likes of *Branded, The Lone Ranger, Laredo,* and *Wagon Train*—as well as the feature films of B Western stalwarts like Roy Rogers, Buck Jones, Wild Bill Elliott, and Johnny Mack Brown—the network offers a revealing glimpse of the nation's video and sociopolitical past.

As it flourished on television, the Western was for a less complicated and less informed era. It was the pastime of a people who trusted more and understood less. If the promise of TV was in part the enlightenment of society through the dissemination of information, the withering of the Western signals a partial achievement of that pledge.

A vestige of an earlier time, the Western has become incompatible with a civilization where the flow of events—especially when exposed through popular television—forced a reevaluation of the innocence and satisfaction with which most Americans had accepted the functioning of their society.

Unlike human mortality, cultural death need not be definitive. While the demise of the Western has been noticeable in the last decade, it may yet enjoy a video renaissance. However, it will never reappear in its older formulations. If ever the genre is to become again a viable form of TV mass entertainment, it must be rebuilt according to new social and intellectual specifications. Among the requirements for the neo-Western on television are the following:

1. It must approach the frontier with believability in depicting the West as an imperfect historical experience in which many gained while many others lost; where Good was a relative term; and where the defeated did not necessarily deserve such a fate. Whether this be accomplished with humor or docudrama frankness, the Western can never again project the American historic past as a flawless process resulting in the triumph of Goodness.

2. It must afford dignity to Asians, Native Americans, Hispanics, Afro-Americans, and other non-Caucasians, for their contributions in the authentic Old West were considerable, and their contemporary constituencies will tolerate no debasing of that record. Where racism existed in the West, it must be shown as a destructive and undesirable perversion that is at least an unfortunate aspect of the fronteir past.

3. Women must be given a respectable role in the frontier experience, not necessarily as gunslingers and bank robbers—although there were women who filled these niches in the real West—but as coequals with men in bringing American society to the hinterland; and in enduring the hurt as well as the triumph of that historic development.

4. The main character in the Western can no longer be depicted as an invincible savior, a metaphorical embodiment of the nation's self-perception. In a time when the limitations of national prowess are popularly understood, there must be analagous weaknesses built into the Western central character that make him or her more recognizably human and vulnerable.

5. Related to the point above, the Western "hero" can no longer be a one-dimensional champion. He or she must demonstrate personal characteristics still appreciated by the mass audience—such traits as self-sacrifice, honorability, intelligence, strength, pride, compassion, and hard work. But the new central character must accept the practical permanence of injustice. Such heroes must measure the completed job against the best of one's abilities, not some mythic perfection that humbles ordinary people.

6. It must remember that while a single motion picture might achieve great popularity, television drama is a recurrent experience. Since TV characters must return each week to regain audience acceptance they must be more comfortable, more honest, and more familiar than movie characterizations.

7. Above all, Western characters must be cognizant of their world and the vital interrelationships within it. There must be respect and dependency between people and their social and natural ecologies. This dignifying relationship must be incorporated into the work of all concerned with crafting the video Western—writers, directors, cinematographers, producers, actors, and others.

8. There may be gimmicks and levity built into the neo-Western, but it still must be relevant to the audience, which is expected to return week after week to its stories; it must respect the critical and intellectual maturity of its audience.

9. While violence must have its place in the neo-Western, it must be timely and nonexploitive. There must be the violence emanating from dramatic conflict, but bloody excess will not be accepted as timely or realistic.

10. The neo-Western must be informational. By using its stories and imagery to communicate matters of social and personal concern, by offering new perspectives on old issues, by demonstrating interesting techniques and physical skills, and by similarly substantial representation, it must fascinate as well as impart understanding to its viewers.

11. It must be crafted with a young audience in mind. Much of contemporary TV viewership is comprised of young people with no roots in the Western. The movie industry has been successful by appealing to teenage tastes; but television producers have a more difficult task: They must make the themes of the Western attractive without turning it into purely teenage entertainment. But first they must introduce the Western to a sizable number of younger viewers who historically have shown little or no interest in the genre.

NOTES

1. Jim Morse, "In Defense of Westerns and Private Eyes," *TV Radio Mirror,* May 1961, p. 70.

2. *TV Guide* (Chicago edition), July 12, 1986, pp. A-1, A-42.

3. *Variety,* June 18, 1986, p. 63.

Bibliography

ARCHIVAL SOURCES

National Broadcasting Company. Records. Madison: Wisconsin State Historical
Society.

UNPUBLISHED SOURCES

King, Margaret Jane. "The Davy Crockett Craze: A Case Study in Popular Culture." Ph.D. dissertation, University of Hawaii, 1976.

Kirkley, Donald Howe Jr. "A Descriptive History of the Network Television
Western during the Seasons 1955-56—1962-63." Ph.D. dissertation, Ohio
University, 1967.

Marsden, Michael. "The Making of *Gunsmoke*: The Writers." Paper delivered at
the 16th Annual Meeting of the Popular Culture Association, Atlanta, April
5, 1986.

Parker, David Willson. "A Descriptive Analysis of The Lone Ranger as a Form of
Popular Art." Ph.D. dissertation, Northwestern University, 1955.

Watson, Mary Ann Rutkowski. "Commercial Television and the New Frontier:
Resistance and Appeasement." Ph.D. dissertation, University of Michigan,
1983.

NEWSPAPERS AND MAGAZINES

Advertising Age
Billboard
Broadcasting
Hollywood Reporter
New York Times
Newsweek
Television
Television Forecast
Television Magazine
Time
TV Guide
Variety

ALMANACS AND VIDEOGRAPHIES

Aaronson, Charles S., ed. *International Television Almanac 1962*. New York:
Quigley Publications, 1961.

Adams, Les, and Buck Rainey. *Shoot-em-Ups: The Complete Reference Guide to Westerns of the Sound Era.* New Rochelle, NY: Arlington House, 1978.

Baily, Kenneth, ed. *The Television Annual for 1959.* London: Odhams Press, 1958.

Brooks, Tim and Earle Marsh. *The Complete Directory to Prime Time Network TV Shows 1946-Present.* New York: Ballantine Books, 1985.

Fredericksson, Kristine. "*Gunsmoke*: Twenty Year Videography." *Journal of Popular Film and Television* XII:1 (Spring 1984), pp. 16-33; XII:2 (Summer 1984), pp. 73-86; XII:3 (Fall 1984), pp. 127-43; XII:4 (Winter 1984/85), pp. 171-86.

Gallup, George S., ed. *The Gallup Poll. Public Opinion 1935-1971.* New York: Random House, 1972.

Gianakos, Larry James, ed. *Television Drama Series Programming: A Comprehensive Chronicle, 1947-1982.* 4 vols. Metuchen, N.J.: Scarecrow Press, 1978-83.

Golenpaul, Ann, ed. *Information Please Almanac 1976.* New York: Dan Golenpaul Associates, 1975.

Hanley, Loretta, ed. *Series, Serials & Packages. A TV Film/Tape Source Book.* New York: Broadcast Information Bureau, 1974.

McNeil, Alex. *Total Television: A Comprehensive Guide to Programming from 1948 to the Present.* New York: Penguin Books, 1984.

Marill, Alvin H., *Movies Made for Television: The Telefeature and the Mini-Series 1964-1984.* New York: New York Zoetrope, 1985.

Terrace, Vincent. *Encyclopedia of Television Series, Pilots and Specials, 1937-1977.* Vol. I. New York: New York Zoetrope, 1986.

Wicking, Christopher, and Tise Vahimagi. *The American Vein. Directors and Directions in Television.* New York: Dutton, 1979.

Woolery, George W. *Children's Television: The First Thirty-Five Years, 1946-1981. Part II: Live, Film, and Tape Series.* (Metuchen, N.J.: Scarecrow Press, 1985).

PRIMARY SOURCES—BOOKS

Abdul-Jabbar, Kareem, and Peter Knobler. *Giant Steps: The Autobiography of Kareem Abdul-Jabbar.* (New York: Bantam, 1983).

Autry, Gene. *Back in the Saddle Again.* New York: Doubleday, 1978.

Fallaci, Oriana. *Interview with History.* Boston: Houghton Mifflin, 1976.

Gruber, Frank. *The Pulp Jungle.* Los Angeles: Sherbourne Press, 1967.

McCoy, Tim, with Ronald McCoy. *Tim McCoy Remembers the West.* Garden City, N.Y.: Doubleday, 1977.

Miner, Worthington. *Worthington Miner.* Metuchen, N.J.: Scarecrow Press, 1985.

PRIMARY SOURCES–ARTICLES

Autry, Gene. "Gene Autry's Prize Round-up." *Radio-Television Mirror,* July 1951, pp. 46, 86.

———. "Producing a Western." *Television Magazine,* October 1952, pp. 25-26.

Conway, Pat. "How I Came to 'Tombstone Territory'." In Baily, Kenneth, ed., *Television Annual for 1959.* London: Odhams Press, 1958.

Gruber, Frank. "The 7 Ways to Plot a Western." *TV Guide,* August 30, 1958, pp. 5-7.

Hargrove, Marion. "This Is a Television Cowboy?" *Life,* January 19, 1959, pp. 73, 75-76.

Huggins, Roy B. "The Bloodshot Eye: A Comment on the Crisis in American Television." *Television Quarterly* 1, no. 3 (August 1962):6-22.

Johnson, Nicholas. "Television and Violence–Perspectives and Proposals." *Television Quarterly* 8, no. 1 (Winter 1969):30-62.

Minow, Newton N. "The Broadcasters Are Public Trustees." In Allen Kirschner and Linda Kirschner, eds. *Radio and Television: Readings in the Mass Media.* Indianapolis: Bobbs-Merrill, 1971, pp. 207-17.

Walker, Clint. "Foreword" to "Meanwhile Back at the Ranch." In *Who's Who in Television and Radio* I:6 (1955):60.

SECONDARY SOURCES–BOOKS

Barbour, Alan G. *Days of Thrills and Adventure.* New York: Collier Books, 1970.

Baritz, Loren. *Backfire: A History of How American Culture Led Us into Vietnam and Made Us Fight the Way We Did.* New York: Morrow, 1985.

Bazin, Andre. *What Is Cinema?* Vol. II. Berkeley: University of California Press, 1971.

Bluem, A. William. *Documentary in Television: Form–Function–Method.* New York: Hastings House, 1965.

Brauer, Ralph. *The Horse, the Gun and the Piece of Property: Changing Images of the TV Western.* Bowling Green, Ohio: Popular Press, 1975.

Calder, Jenni. *There Must Be a Lone Ranger: The American West in Film and in Reality.* New York: Taplinger, 1975.

Cawelti, John G. *The Six-Gun Mystique.* 2nd ed. Bowling Green, Ohio: Popular Press, 1984.

Comstock, George A., and Steve Chaffee et al. *Television and Human Behavior.* New York: Columbia University Press, 1975.

Durham, Philip. *The Negro Cowboys.* New York: Dodd, Mead, 1965.

Fenin, George, and William K. Everson. *The Western from Silents to Cinerama.* New York: Orion Press, 1962.

Fiedler, Leslie A. *The Return of the Vanishing American.* New York: Stein and Day, 1968.

French, Philip. *Westerns: Aspects of a Movie Genre.* New York: Viking Press, 1973.

Friar, Ralph E., and Natasha A. Friar. *The Only Good Indian . . . The Hollywood Gospel.* New York: Drama Book Specialists, 1972.

Furhammar, Leif, and Folke Isaksson. *Politics and Film.* New York: Praeger, 1968 and 1971.

Gitlin, Todd. *Inside Prime Time.* New York: Pantheon Books, 1983.

Glut, Donald F., and Jim Harmon. *The Great Television Heroes.* Garden City, N.Y.: Doubleday, 1975.

Goldsen, Rose K. *The Show and Tell Machine: How Television Works and Works You Over.* New York: Dial Press, 1977.

Grossman, Gary H. *Saturday Morning TV.* New York: Dell, 1981.

Himmelstein, Hal. *Television Myth and the American Mind.* New York: Praeger Publishers, 1984.

Horwitz, James. *They Went Thataway.* New York: Ballantine Books, 1978.

Hyams, Jay. *The Life and Times of the Western Movie.* Bromley, England: Columbia Books, 1983.

Katz, William Loren. *The Black West.* New York: Anchor Books, 1973.

Lacourbe, Roland. *La guerre froide dans le cinema d'espionnage.* Paris. Editions Henri Veyrier, 1985.

_____. *Nazisme et seconde guerre mondiale dans le cinema d'espionnage.* Paris: Editions Henri Veyrier, 1983.

Lenihan, John H. *Showdown: Confronting Modern America in the Western Film.* Urbana: University of Illinois Press, 1980.

MacDonald, J. Fred. *Blacks and White TV: Afro-Americans in Television since 1948.* Chicago: Nelson-Hall, 1983.

_____. *Don't Touch That Dial! Radio Programming in American Life, 1920-1960.* Chicago: Nelson-Hall, 1979.

_____. *Television and the Red Menace: The Video Road to Vietnam.* New York: Praeger, 1985.

Maltin, Leonard. *The Disney Films.* New York: Crown, 1973.

Miller, Don. *Hollywood Corral.* New York: Popular Library, 1976.

Newcomb, Horace. *TV: The Most Popular Art.* Garden City, N.Y.: Doubleday, 1974.

Newcomb, Horace, and Robert S. Alley. *The Producer's Medium. Conversations with Creators of American TV.* New York: Oxford University Press, 1983.

Rothel, David. *Who Was That Masked Man? The Story of the Lone Ranger.* South Brunswick, N.J.: A.S. Barnes, 1976.

Schatz, Thomas. *Hollywood Genres: Formulas, Filmmaking, and the Studio System.* Philadelphia: Temple University Press, 1981.

Schickel, Richard. *The Disney Version: The Life, Times, Art, and Commerce of Walt Disney.* New York: Simon and Schuster, 1968.

Seydor, Paul. *Peckinpah: The Western Films.* Urbana: University of Illinois Press, 1980.

Simmons, Garner. *Peckinpah: A Portrait in Montage.* Austin: University of Texas Press, 1982.

Smith, Henry Nash. *Virgin Land: The American West As Symbol and Myth.* Cambridge, Mass.: Harvard University Press, 1950.

Smith, Julian. *Looking Away: Hollywood and Vietnam.* New York: Charles Scribner's Sons, 1975.

Turner, Frederick Jackson. *The Frontier in American History.* New York: Henry Holt, 1947.

United States Commission on Civil Rights. *Window Dressing on the Set. Women and Minorities in Television.* Washington, D.C.: U.S. Government Printing Office, 1977.

Viviani, Christian. *Le western.* Paris: Editions Henri Veyrier, 1982.

Wilson, Clint C. II, and Felix Gutierrez. *Minorities and Media: Diversity and the End of Mass Communication.* (Beverly Hills, Calif.: Sage Publications, 1985).

Wright, Will. *Six Guns and Society: A Structural Study of the Western.* Berkeley: University of California Press, 1975.

SECONDARY SOURCES—ARTICLES

Amory, Cleveland. "Review: *The Dakotas.*" *TV Guide,* April 6, 1963, p. 1.

————. "Review: *The Legend of Jesse James.*" *TV Guide,* April 30, 1966, p. 1.

Clepper, P. M. "Some Advice to the Producers of *Custer.*" *TV Guide,* September 23, 1967, pp. 32-34.

Davidson, Bill. "Walt Disney: The Latter-Day Aesop." *TV Guide,* May 20, 1961, pp. 24-27.

Durham, Philip. "The Negro Cowboy." In Hennig Cohen, ed., *The American Experience: Approaches to the Study of the United States.* Boston: Houghton Mifflin, 1968, pp. 259-69.

Ellis, Robert P. "The Appeal of the Western Movie Thriller." *America,* May 17, 1958, pp. 228-29.

Evans, John W. "Modern Man and the Cowboy." *Television Quarterly* 1, no. 2 (May 1962):31-41.

Field, Eunice. "How a Western Is Made." *TV Radio Mirror,* May 1959, pp. 44-47, 73.

————. "Wanted—Very Much Alive." *TV Radio Mirror,* April 1959, pp. 54-57, 61.

Hastings, Charles. "The War of the Cowboys." *Motion Picture Magazine*, November 1947, pp. 44-45, 85-87.

Homans, Peter. "Puritanism Revisited: An Analysis of the Contemporary Screen-Image Western." *Studies in Public Communication,* Summer 1961, pp. 73-84.

————. "The Western. The Legend and the Cardboard Hero." *Look,* March 13, 1962, pp. 82-90.

Jacobson, Herbert L. "Cowboy, Pioneer and American Soldier." *Sight and Sound,* April-June 1953, pp. 189-90.

Jensen, Oliver. "Hopalong Hits the Jackpot." *Life,* June 12, 1950, pp. 63-68, 70.

Johnson, Bob. "Why 'Maverick' Spurns the Code of the Westerns." *TV Guide,* August 1, 1959, pp. 17-19.

Kelsay, Bill. "Clu Gulager." *TV Radio Mirror,* December 1960, pp. 44-45, 67-68.

Land, Herman. "After the Western—What?" *Television Magazine,* July 1958, pp. 55-57.

Lardner, John. "Decline and Fall Possible." *The New Yorker,* February 28, 1959, pp. 97-100.

————. "The Hybrid Western." *The New Yorker,* January 18, 1958, pp. 86-89; January 25, 1958, pp. 64-68.

Lyle, J., and H. R. Hoffman. "Children's Use of Television and Other Media." In E. A. Rubinstein, George A. Comstock, and J. P. Murray, eds., *Television and Social Behavior,* Vol. IV: *Television in Day-to-Day Life: Patterns of Use.* Washington, D.C.: U.S. Government Printing Office, 1972, pp. 129-256.

McBride, Jeff. "The Man Who Stole His Life." *TV Radio Mirror,* January 1964, pp. 38-39, 64, 86-87.

MacKenzie, Robert. "Review: *The Quest.*" *TV Guide,* October 30, 1976, p. 34.

McMurtry, Larry. "Cowboys, Movies, Myths, and Cadillacs: Realism in the Western." In W. R. Robinson, ed., *Man and the Movies.* Baton Rouge: University of Louisiana Press, 1967, pps. 46-52.

Miller, Alexander. "The Western—A Theological Note." *The Christian Century,* November 27, 1957, pp. 1409-10.

Morhaim, Joe. "Why *Gunsmoke*'s Amanda Blake, Jim Arness Won't Kiss." *TV Guide,* March 15, 1958, pp. 8-11.

Morse, Jim. "In Defense of Westerns and Private Eyes." *TV Radio Mirror,* May 1961, pp. 18-19, 70-71.

Morse, Leon. "Hubbell Robinson Evaluates TV Programming Today." *Television Magazine,* December 1959, pp. 48-51.

Nussbaum, Martin. "Sociological Symbolism in the 'Adult Western.'" *Social Forces,* October 1960, pp. 25-28.

Peck, Richard E. "Films, Television, and Tennis." In W. R. Robinson, ed., *Man and the Movies.* Baton Rouge: University of Louisiana Press, 1967, pp. 97-111.

Reddy, John. "TV Westerns: The Shots Heard Round the World." *Reader's Digest,* January 1959, pp. 134-36.

Remenih, Maurine. "No Rings around Ringo." *TV Radio Mirror,* May 1960, pp. 48-51, 77-78.

Rickenbacker, William F. "60,000,000 Westerners Can't Be Wrong." *National Review,* October 23, 1962, pp. 322-25.

Sisk, John P. "The Western Hero." *Commonweal,* July 12, 1957, pp. 367-69.

Teeple, David Shea. "TV Westerns Tell a Story." *The American Mercury,* April 1958, pp. 115-17.

White, Peter T. "Ex-King of the Wild Frontier." New York *Times Magazine,* December 11, 1955, p. 27.

Whitney, Dwight. "The Taming of the West—and *The Californians*—by Memo." *TV Guide,* September 13, 1958, pp. 8-11.

————. "What's *Gunsmoke*'s Secret?" *TV Guide,* August 22, 1970, pp. 20-25.

————. "Why 'Gunsmoke' Keeps Blazing." *TV Guide,* December 6, 1958, pp. 8-11.

Index

About the Author

J. Fred MacDonald is a recognized authority on the social and cultural history of the mass media. His articles have appeared in journals such as *American Quarterly, Journal of Popular Culture, Journal of Popular Film and Television, Phylon,* and *Advertising Age.* He is the author of three previous books: *Don't Touch That Dial! Radio Programming in American Life, 1920-1960* (1979); *Blacks and White TV: Afro-Americans in Television since 1948* (1983); and with Praeger Publishers *Television and the Red Menace: The Video Road to Vietnam* (1985). He is also a past president of the Popular Culture Association.

Dr. MacDonald holds B.A. and M.A. degrees in history from the University of California at Berkeley, and a Ph.D. in history from the University of California at Los Angeles.

Dr. MacDonald is professor of history at Northeastern Illinois University in Chicago. He is also general editor of the Media and Society series published by Praeger Publishers. He is curator of the Museum of Broadcast Communications located in Chicago.